T0059503

TOKYO
Like a Local

BY THE PEOPLE WHO CALL IT HOME

TOKYO
Like a Local

BY THE PEOPLE WHO CALL IT HOME

Contents

EAT

DRINK

SHOP

ARTS & CULTURE

NIGHTLIFE

OUTDOORS

meet the locals

LUCY DAYMAN

Australian-born Lucy moved to Japan in 2016 for what she thought would be a working holiday, but fast-forward to today, and she still hasn't left (Tokyo does that to a person). When she's not working – as a travel consultant, writer, and co-founder of a creative agency – Lucy spends time cycling through less-trodden streets and taking film photos (the kind you have to develop) with admittedly mixed results.

KAILA IMADA

A Japanese-Canadian writer and editor at Time Out Tokyo, Kaila moved to Tokyo in 2017 to get in touch with her Japanese side, and has been a Tokyoite ever since. She loves discovering new corners of Tokyo, always in the hope of hunting down the best ramen in the city and chancing upon offbeat art galleries.

Tokyo
WELCOME TO THE CITY

To call Tokyo a city is to do it a disservice. It's a mega city, built from a hundred tiny cities, layer upon layer, story upon story. This is a place where 100-year-old family-run cafés share real estate with avant-garde sneaker pop-ups. Turn a corner and you'll chance upon an Edo-era suburb where tea masters uphold traditional ceremonies; mere steps away will be a neon-drenched alley where anime fans spend days immersed in fantasy worlds.

Tokyo is a place where subcultures reign, each of its million's of inhabitants making their mark – be it the kawaii cosplay girls of Harajuku, the fashionistas of Omotesando, or the salarymen of Shinbashi. But no matter how different Tokyoites appear on the surface, they all share a humble sense of pride for how far they've come. This is a place that's had its fair share of cultural censorship and devastations, but it celebrates self-expression and looks fearlessly into the future like nowhere else.

It's easy to see why, then, Japan has captured the world's imagination. You're obsessed, we're obsessed, everyone's obsessed – but if you really want to get under the skin of Tokyo, you need to go via the locals, and that's where this book comes in. The locals are the ones writing this mega city's story, providing the endless layers that make up its very heart – like the baker crafting handmade bread every morning, the gallerist curating the latest photography show, and the rockstar keeping moshpits alive at underground venues. After all, Tokyo isn't all bright lights and traditional temples; rather, this is a place that always finds a way to surprise you.

So, come to Tokyo with an open mind, the expectation that your expectations will be challenged, and the knowledge that you'll never be able to have "done" Tokyo, and you'll enjoy it to its fullest. Oh, and sleep? Save that for the train commute – you won't want to waste a second.

Liked by the locals

"Tokyo may seem intimidating on first glance, but past the elaborate train system and streets bustling with people, you'll find that the city is welcoming and affectionate, making you feel right at home."

KAILA IMADA, WRITER AND EDITOR

Life in Tokyo centers around the four seasons, and traditions shape each one – cherry blossom parties in the spring to hot-spring soaks in the fall.

Tokyo

THROUGH THE YEAR

SPRING

CHERRY BLOSSOM TIME
Marking the transition from winter to spring is a riot of pink sakura across Tokyo. Locals celebrate with *hanami*, cherry-blossom viewing picnics beneath the blooming trees.

SPORT SPECTACULAR
Sumo season hits its peak in May, when the anticipated Tokyo Grand Sumo Tournament is held. Those lucky enough to get a ticket cheer at the stadium, but most gather at home to watch it on TV.

SPRING DELICACIES
Japanese food is heavily influenced by the seasons, and spring is a time of new growth. Restaurants swap out heavy winter food for lighter flavors: think bamboo shoots, fresh sea bream, and sakura-flavored sweets and drinks.

SUMMER

TRADITIONAL FESTIVITIES
Summer starts with a bang – literally – when *hanabi* (fireworks) season lights up the sky. Donning a *yukata* (summer kimono), dancing through the streets, and tucking into street food defines the rest of the festival season, full of celebrations for everything from deities to flowers.

COOLING DOWN
Sighs of *"atsui!"* ("it's hot!") and tinklings of wind chimes make up the sounds of summer. Hot, humid days in the city are made bearable with *kakigori* (a shaved

ice dessert). But when the heat gets too much, locals head to seaside towns for a dose of cooler air and a refreshing dip.

MUSIC FESTIVALS
Musicians of every genre take over in the summer. Fuji Rock brings, well, rock in July; Summer Sonic plays a mix of punk, rock, and hip-hop in August; and Ultra Japan gets crowds pumping to electronic dance music in September.

FALL

LEAFY WALKS
Koyo (fall leaves) come to the fore and cause an obsession similar to spring's cherry blossoms. Most people stroll through the parks to enjoy the colors, but the more adventurous head to the mountains.

BATH TIME
As the days get colder, Tokyoites head into traditional bathhouses or venture to hot-spring towns to warm up and relax.

HALLOWEEN HAPPENINGS
People here need little excuse to dress up (Tokyo is cosplay central, after all) and Halloween is unsurprisingly big

business come October. Partygoers take to the streets in extravagant costumes for epic parties.

WINTER

MARKETS GALORE
Stunning illuminations mark the start of winter across the city. Locals wrap up and head to holiday markets, stocking up on gifts and delicious treats. Perusing the 700-odd stalls at the Setagaya Boroichi flea market is a yearly ritual.

GETTING COSY
With darker nights and a chill in the air, it's all about indulging in winter warmers: comforting *oden* (stew), *nabe* (hot pots), and hot sake.

HITTING THE SLOPES
Ski season is a big deal in Japan, but as Tokyo lacks the requisites for winter sports, groups take the train to nearby ski villages for weekend fun.

NEW YEAR'S EVE
A new year in Tokyo is a time to reflect – and party. Some locals head to temples to pray for good health while others celebrate at clubs.

There's an art to being a local in Tokyo, where unspoken rules guide every interaction – from greeting others to dining out. Here we offer a starting point.

Tokyo
KNOW-HOW

For a directory of health and safety resources, safe spaces, and accessibility information, turn to page 186. For everything else, read on.

Japan is *big* on manners, and a run-through of social customs could easily fill a book in itself (chopstick rules alone are endless). Our advice? Once you've got to grips with the basics here, carry on the research. Getting things wrong can cause offence, and we don't want that.

EAT

Mealtimes are sacred in Tokyo. Most folk eat breakfast at home, so places tend to open at lunch, around 11:30am. Dinner is the biggest meal of the day, and many spots close between 2:30 and 5:30pm to prepare. As dining times are limited, you'll need to reserve ahead – oh, and if you're veggie or vegan, say so. Hungry between meals? Hit up a convenience store.

DRINK

The city's drinking scene generally falls into two extremes: rustic old-school spots and hip modern joints. Most people get their teas and coffees at cool cafés, but vending machines with bottled bevs are a blessing when you're on-the-go.

When it comes to alcohol, after-work drinks are the done thing. Not so common? Pouring your own drink. It's impolite, so always pour for others, wait for them to return the favor, and only drink once everyone is served. Kick things off with a toast of *kampai* (cheers).

SHOP

Wherever you shop, politeness is the golden rule. So, smile when you enter a store, follow changing-room rules (like leaving your shoes outside), and whatever you do, don't bargain (unless you're at a flea market). Most shops and malls open at around 10am, and close late, at 8pm. Oh, and carry an eco-bag to avoid a ¥5 charge for one.

ARTS & CULTURE

Museums come at a cost: literally (few are free) and physically (they're packed on the weekend). Save your visits for a weekday or exhibition – though these get booked up weeks ahead, so get planning.

Got theater tickets? There's no need to dress up (forgo your ripped jeans, mind). There is, however, a need for silence: don't drink or eat, and only clap once the performers have left the stage.

NIGHTLIFE

With last trains around 1am – and venues open until much later – most folk stay out until the first train at 5am. Clubs don't hit their peak until 2am anyway, so the hours before pass in *izakaya* or karaoke joints.

Many locals swap clubbing for a night at a bathhouse. Got a tattoo? They're not always welcome, or might need covering. Clothes are also not allowed, but baths are gender-segregated, and everyone washes before entering.

OUTDOORS

Tokyoites have a strong love for nature, especially in spring when cherry blossom picnics are ritualistic. The places you

shouldn't picnic? Around shrines and temples – it's offensive. Locals take good care of their city (it's pretty clean), so do the same. You'll rarely find garbage cans out and about, so take your trash home to dispose of.

Keep in mind

Here are some more tips and tidbits that will help you fit in like a local.

» **Cash is king** Many small venues don't accept credit cards, so keep cash on you. Don't hand it to the cashier; place it in a money tray.

» **No smoking** Lighting up is banned indoors and on the streets in central Tokyo. However, some restaurants allow it – there's usually a sign at the entrance.

» **Don't tip** Tipping is considered offensive. Instead, some venues may apply a service charge.

» **Shoes off, please** It's custom to take off your shoes when entering a home or sacred building, and when sitting on tatami mats.

GETTING AROUND

Tokyo is divided into a whopping 23 wards (council districts) as well as 39 other municipalities, which include cities, towns, and villages. The famous sights you'll be most familiar with are located in the central wards, which spread around the Tokyo Bay area. We'll level with you: Tokyo's address system can be complex, and finding lesser-known sights a struggle, as only main thoroughfares tend to have street names. In an address – for example, "2-3-4 Otemachi" – the first number refers to the chome (main block), the second a smaller block of buildings within the chome, and the last an even smaller block of buildings.

To make your life easier we've provided what3words addresses for each sight in this book, meaning you can quickly pinpoint exactly where you're heading with ease.

On foot

For a city as big as Tokyo, it's surprisingly walkable – in fact, walking is the best way to get a feel for each neighborhood (p14). That being said, there are some key rules to follow. Central Tokyo is known for its frenetic energy, so stay to the left on sidewalks. Sidewalks can also get pretty packed, so don't stop in the middle of foot traffic or you'll get pushed.

If you do need to check a what3words address, find a quiet place to stop. Oh, and *never* eat while walking – it's rude.

On wheels

Cycling is one of the fastest ways to get around, but it's also just a nice way – especially through back alleys and quiet streets. You may notice people cycling on the sidewalk, but make sure you stick to the road (this is the only time we'll advise you not to do as the locals do). Some major streets have designated bike lanes, but if not, just follow car traffic.

Bike rentals are becoming pretty common. The Tokyo Bicycle Sharing program is popular, and operates in ten of the central wards. The red-and-black e-bikes are easy to spot, and there are 650 ports in the city – simply register as a member online beforehand. Though usage fees vary by area, a single use costs around ¥150 for the first half hour, and a one-day pass costs ¥1,500. *www.docomo-cycle.jp*

By public transportation

Tokyo's public transportation system can seem overwhelming when first glancing at a subway map, but it's incredibly easy to use, and people are very helpful. Plus, it's one of the most efficient in the world – it's equipped to handle over 10 million people every day, after all. Nonetheless, this leads to an incredibly busy rush hour. If you're thinking of braving the daily crush, follow the golden rules: don't eat, avoid loud conversations, and hold your backpack in front of you to make space for others.

One-way tickets can be purchased for trains, but the easiest way to get around is with a prepaid IC card (a Suica or Pasmo) that can be used on virtually all forms of transportation in Tokyo and surrounding areas. The cards can be bought and reloaded at stations, convenience stores, and on buses. At train stations and on city buses, tap in on departure then out when exiting.

By car or taxi

Driving in Tokyo can be a pain: roads are clogged with traffic and rental cars tend to feature Japanese-only sat nav systems. If you really do need to drive, check out the Japan Automobile Federation (JAF) for details about rentals.

Taxis lean on the pricier side, and there's a late-night surcharge if you're taking one between 10pm and 5am. However, Tokyo's cabbies are top-notch – JapanTaxi's app is the best way to find one. Just make sure you have an address in Japanese you can show them.
www.jaf.or.jp

Download these

We recommend you download these apps to help you get about the city.

WHAT3WORDS
Your geocoding friend
A what3words address is a simple way to communicate any precise location on earth, using just three words. ///glides.clock.waiters, for example, is the code for Meiji Shrine. Simply download the free what3words app, type a what3words address into the search bar, and you'll know exactly where to go.

HYPERDIA
Your local transportation service
Tokyo's rail network consists of trains run by JR East and other private companies such as Tokyo Metro, Toei Subway, and Seibu Railway, which also runs the city's public buses. This travel-planning app provides up-to-date information for the whole lot.

*Tokyo is home to distinct wards and neighborhoods,
each with their own local charm and community.
Here we take a look at some of our favorites.*

Tokyo
NEIGHBORHOODS

Akihabara

Tokyo's "electric town" is a hot spot for all things *otaku* (geek), where self-confessed nerds shop for anime goods and techies pick up their gadgets. {map 3}

Asakusa

Old Tokyo vibes live on here, with centuries-old craft stalls and the city's oldest temple, Sensoji, giving a window into the past. {map 3}

Daikanyama

It's odd to think this was once an archaeological site, given how modern it is today. Now, chic locals and trendy celebs rave about the classy boutiques and alfresco sidewalk cafés. {map 4}

Ebisu

Known for its enviable (read: pricey) apartments, Ebisu is upscale but laid-back – helped, no doubt, by the community of expats and long-timers who take it easy in the standing bars and cosy pubs. {map 4}

Ginza

Fashion doesn't get more high-end than in Ginza – the Mayfair of Tokyo. Luxury department stores have long attracted suited-and-booted professionals to shop in this part of the city. {map 5}

Harajuku

This was the heartland of alternative street style in the 1990s (think vibrant *kawaii*

and punk looks), but most shoppers wear more global brands here these days. That said, Harajuku remains an epicenter of experimental fashion, where Tokyo's youth come to find unique clothes to express themselves. {map 1}

Ikebukuro

Sorry Akihabara, you've got competition. Ikebukuro is buzzy, geeky, and teems with large stores aimed particularly at anime and manga fangirls. {map 6}

Koenji

Sleepy Koenji is cool, liberal, and grungy – much like the musicians and artists who call it home. Its live music scene and record stores can't be beaten. {map 6}

Nakameguro

This area is as eclectic as its locals. Taprooms attract hipsters, high-end boutiques draw the wealthy (groomed pups in tow), and the Meguro River is a family favorite – especially during cherry blossom season. *{map 4}*

Nakano

This area is often defined by its geek-centric mall, Nakano Broadway, but Nakano's foodie scene is where it's at. Beloved *izakaya* and top-notch ramen restaurants await here. *{map 2}*

Nihonbashi

The city's commercial hub for centuries, Nihonbashi is home to some of the world's oldest businesses, from bank headquarters in ultramodern buildings to tiny kimono shops. *{map 3}*

Odaiba

When locals want to escape the center, they retreat to this artificial island. Aside from its "beach," Odaiba has quirky museums and amusement parks – perfect for teens and families. *{map 5}*

Roppongi

As famed for its art scene as its nightlife, Roppongi is constantly buzzing. By day, creatives flock to its Art Triangle; the night owls among them stay on for the epic club scene. *{map 5}*

Ryogoku

Tokyo's sumo town has long been the center of the sport, and people still journey across the city to catch a game or watch the wrestlers at the sumo stables. *{map 3}*

Shibuya

If you had to pick a stock image of Tokyo, it would show Shibuya Crossing – crowds and high-rises galore. Always abuzz, this neon-lit area has been the party town for Tokyo's youth since the 1930s. *{map 4}*

Shimokitazawa

Since the city's creative youth settled here in the 1980s, it's been known as "alternative Tokyo." You can hardly move for baseball cap-clad hipsters thrift shopping and sipping coffee. *{map 4}*

Shinjuku

This is frenetic Tokyo at its best. Between skyscrapers, the streets buzz with people shopping, ducking into the world's busiest train station, and partying in Asia's largest LGBTQ+ district. *{map 2}*

Tomigaya

Fast-gentrifying but still dedicated to tradition, this area is loved for its hip design stores and serene village feel. It's no wonder journalists call it one of the coolest places to live. *{map 2}*

Yanaka

Traditional Tokyo at its best, Yanaka is full of glimpses into the Edo era. Not only is it home to Tokyo's oldest architecture (it avoided WWII bombings), its narrow streets are lined with shops owned by the same family for generations. *{map 3}*

Yoyogi-Uehara

A village-like, multicultural area, with strong Turkish and Arab communities, Yoyogi-Uehara is awash with fab restaurants serving up global grub. *{map 2}*

Tokyo
ON THE MAP

Whether you're looking for your new favorite spot or want to check out what each part of Tokyo has to offer, our maps – along with handy map references throughout the book – have you covered.

KAWAGOE

6

TOKOROZAWA

Shingashi

Tama Lake

TACHIKAWA

AKISHMA

Tama River

FUCHU

CHUO EXPRESSWA

HACHIOJI

HINO

SAGIMAHARA

Tsurumi River

MACHIDA

Sagami River

Onda River

ATSUGI

YAMATO

0 kilometers 5

0 miles 5

EBINA

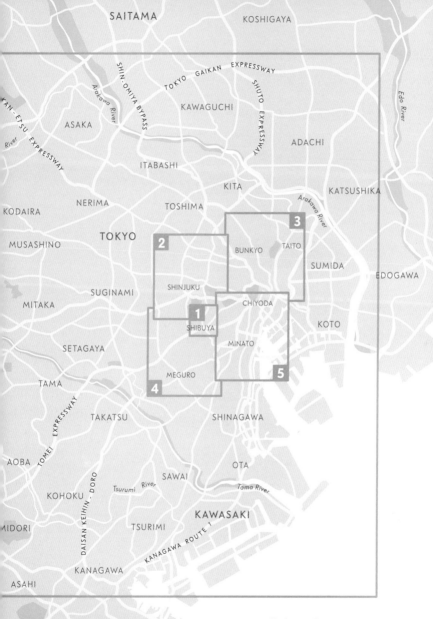

SHIBUYA

Yoyogi Park

Togo Shrine **D**

TAKESHITA-DORI

MEIJI - DORI

JINGUMAE

HARAJUKU

Gonpachi
Nori-Temaki **E**

Kinji **S** **S** Neighborhood

INOKASHIRA - DORI

FIRE - DORI

Sankey's
Penthouse **N**

OMOTESANDO - DORI

Menchirashi **S** **S** Number Sugar
Ragtag

MEIJI - DORI

JINNAN

JINGUMAE

Kaitensushi
Ginza Onodera **E**

INOKASHIRA - DORI

D The SG Club

Kidoguchi

Sakurai **D** **E**

Whisky
Library **D**

Gen Gen An
by En Tea

Manhattan Records **S** **D**

Nintendo Store **S** **N** Izakaya Masaka

AOYAMA - DORI

KOEN-DORI

Takkyu Sakaba Ponzo **N**

N WWW
N KitKat
Karaoke   Chocolatory
Kan   **S**

Viron **E**

SHOTO

UDAGAWACHO

Grandfather's
D   **D** Bloody Angle Dougen Tong
Satei Hato

Village
Vanguard **S**

MIYAMASU-ZAKA

Ryukyu
Chinese Tama

N

SAKAE-DORI

Ruby Room **N**
Lion **D**   **N** **E** Uobei
Uogashi Nihon-ichi **E**

Gyukatsu **E**
Motomura

Nonbei
Yokocho **N**

SHIBUYA

Aoyama Tunnel **D** **N** Aoyama Hachi

Lighthouse Records **S**

A Tokyo Comedy Bar

ROPPONGI - DORI

EXPRESSWAY NO. 3

Womb **N** **N**
Harlem

OATH **N** **N** Zubar
E

Pokémon **S**
Center

D Bar Ishinohana

MEIJI - DORI

MARUYAMACHO

DOGEN-
ZAKA

Parfaiteria
Bel

Sushi **E**
Tokyo Ten

DOGEN-
ZAKA   TAMAGAWA-DORI

SHIBUYA RIVER

EXPRESSWAY NO. 3

SAKURA-
GAOKACHO

HIGASHI

SHIBUYA

Shibuya River

0 meters   400
0 yards   400

UGUISUDANICHO

HACHIMAN-DORI

MAP 1

1

MAP 2

2

SEKIGUCHI

MEJIRO - DORI

WASEDAMACHI

Yayoi Kusama **A**
Museum

BENTENCHO

YOCHOMACHI

YASUKUNI - DORI

SANEICHO

SHINJUKU - DORI

SHINANOMACHI

Meiji Jingu
⊃ Stadium

A TEPIA

Aoyama
Cemetery

MINAMI-
OYAMA

ROPPONGI

E EAT

Bake Cheese Tart *(p54)*
Florilège *(p46)*
Fukuho Gyoza *(p40)*
Haritts Donuts & Coffee *(p53)*
Levain *(p48)*
Path *(p49)*
Sio *(p44)*
Yakitori Imai *(p46)*

D DRINK

Ahiru Store *(p69)*
Lug *(p68)*
Sanita *(p70)*
Sansan *(p70)*
Yona Yona Beer Works *(p65)*
Y.Y.G. Brewery & Beer
    Kitchen *(p67)*
Zoetrope *(p75)*

S SHOP

Big Love Records *(p91)*
Disk Union Shinjuku *(p90)*
Nakano Broadway *(p97)*

A ARTS &
CULTURE

Japan National Stadium *(p131)*
Meiji Jingu Stadium *(p130)*

Nanzuka *(p112)*
Red Bull Gaming Sphere
    Tokyo *(p130)*
TEPIA *(p118)*
Yayoi Kusama Museum *(p115)*

N NIGHTLIFE

Aisotope Lounge *(p148)*
Arty Farty *(p150)*
Bonobo *(p150)*
Daikoku-Yu *(p154)*
Golden Gai *(p138)*
Hachiman-Yu *(p155)*
New Sazae *(p151)*
Omoide Yokocho *(p139)*
Oslo Batting Center *(p157)*
Sasazuka Bowl *(p159)*
Thermae-Yu *(p152)*

O OUTDOORS

Meiji Shrine *(p177)*
Mejiro Garden *(p167)*
Shinjuku Gyoen National
    Garden *(p166)*
Yoyogi Park *(p168)*

0 kilometers 1
0 miles 1

E Onigiri Bongo

KOMAGOME

ORIDO - DORI

HAKUSAN - DORI

HONGO - DORI

TABATA

SHINOBAZU - DORI

HIGASHI-TABATA

MEIJI - DORI

ARAKAWA

ARAKAWA

NISHI-NIPPORI

OGUBASHI-DORI

O Rikugien Gardens

MINAMI-OTSUKA

SENGOKU

HONKOMAGOME

E Himitsudo

SENDAGI

HIGASHI-NIPPORI

YANAKA

Yanaka Cemetery

Otsuka Park

SHINOBAZU - DORI

SENKAWA - DORI

Koishikawa Botanical Garden

HAKUSAN

KYU-HAKUSAN-DORI

O Nezu Shrine

NEZU

Scai the Bathhouse **A** **E** Vaner

KOTOTOI - DORI

UENO-SAKURAGI

KASUGA - DORI

OTSUKA

KASUGA - DORI

BUNKYO

KOISHIKAWA

NISHIKATA

HAKUSAN - DORI

HONGO - DORI

Tokyo Metropolitan Art Museum **A**

KITA-UENO

TAITO

KOHINATA

HONGO

University of Tokyo

SHINOBAZU-DORI

O Ueno Park

HIGASHI-UENO

KASUGA

UENO

Ameya-Yokocho **N**

AKAGISHITAMACHI

EXPRESSWAY NO. 5

WASEDA - DORI

O Akagi Shrine

Akomeya **S**

YARAICHO

Tokyo Dome **A** Spa LaQua **N**

KORAKU

Korakuen Hall **A**

Space Museum TeNQ **A**

Kanda River

YUSHIMA

SOTOKANDA

Game Bar A-Button **N**

EXPRESSWAY NO. 1

TAITO

KAGURAZAKA

FUJIMI

OKUBO-DORI

MEJIRO-DORI

Nihonbashi River

Meishu Center **D**

AKB48 Theater **N**

AKIHABARA

ASAKUSA-BASHI

SHINJUKU

SOTOBORI-DORI

Soto-dori

KUDAN-KITA

KANDA-JINBOCHO

YASUKUNI - DORI

KANDA

Dine on a Yakatabune **C**

ICHIGAYA

O Yasukuni Shrine

A Nippon Budokan

Kitanomaru Park

KANDA-NISHIKICHO

UCHI-KANDA

IWAMOTOCHO

HIGASHI-NIHONBAS

YONBANCHO

O Imperial Palace East Gardens

OTEMACHI

NIHONBASHI-NINGYOCHO

KOJIMACHI

O Row down Chidorigafuchi Moat

CHIYODA

SHINJUKU-DORI

HIRAKAWACHO

Mitsukoshi Nihombashi **S**

HONGO-DORI

Kayanoya **S**

CHUO

NIHONBASHI

CHIYODA

EXPRESSWAY NO. 4

NAGATACHO

YAESU

Nanahari **N**

SHINKAWA

MAP 3

🅔 EAT

Bon *(p46)*
Himitsudo *(p53)*
Onigiri Bongo *(p41)*
Suzukien Asakusa *(p54)*
Vaner *(p48)*

🅓 DRINK

Arise Coffee Roasters *(p76)*
Meishu Center *(p73)*

🅢 SHOP

Akomeya *(p92)*
Kayanoya *(p93)*
Mitsukoshi Nihombashi *(p94)*

🅐 ARTS & CULTURE

Arashio-Beya Sumo Stable *(p129)*
Korakuen Hall *(p129)*
Nippon Budokan *(p130)*
Ryogoku Kokugikan *(p128)*
Scai the Bathhouse *(p113)*
Space Museum TeNQ *(p119)*
Tokyo Dome *(p131)*
Tokyo Metropolitan Art
Museum *(p113)*

🅝 NIGHTLIFE

AKB48 Theater *(p145)*
Ameya-Yokocho *(p137)*
Game Bar A-Button *(p156)*
Nanahari *(p146)*
Ryogoku Edo-Yu *(p152)*
Spa LaQua *(p153)*

🅞 OUTDOORS

Akagi Shrine *(p176)*
Dine on a Yakatabune *(p175)*
Imperial Palace East
Gardens *(p164)*
Nezu Shrine *(p178)*
Rikugien Gardens *(p165)*
Row down Chidorigafuchi
Moat *(p173)*
Sensoji Temple *(p176)*
Ueno Park *(p170)*
Yasukuni Shrine *(p178)*

MAP 4

MAP 5

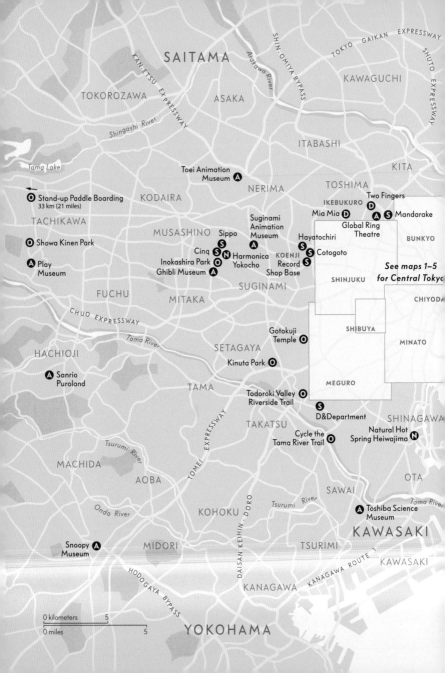

MAP 6

6

ADACHI

Arakawa River

'AITO

D Himekura

SUMIDA

O Run the Arakawa River Trail

O Kiba Park

KOTO

Tokyo Bay

D DRINK

Himekura *(p75)*

Mia Mia *(p78)*

Two Fingers *(p67)*

S SHOP

Cinq *(p100)*

Cotogoto *(p103)*

D&Department *(p103)*

Hayatochiri *(p106)*

Mandarake *(p96)*

Record Shop Base *(p88)*

Sippo *(p102)*

A ARTS & CULTURE

Ghibli Museum *(p121)*

Global Ring Theatre *(p127)*

Play Museum *(p118)*

Sanrio Puroland *(p123)*

Snoopy Museum *(p123)*

Suginami Animation Museum *(p123)*

Toei Animation Museum *(p120)*

Toshiba Science Museum *(p119)*

N NIGHTLIFE

Harmonica Yokocho *(p137)*

Natural Hot Spring Heiwajima *(p154)*

O OUTDOORS

Run the Arakawa River Trail *(p172)*

Cycle the Tama River Trail *(p175)*

Gotokuji Temple *(p179)*

Inokashira Park *(p168)*

Kiba Park *(p170)*

Kinuta Park *(p170)*

Showa Kinen Park *(p171)*

Stand-up Paddle Boarding *(p172)*

Todoroki Valley Riverside Trail *(p173)*

EAT

Tokyo's vast food scene goes far beyond sushi joints, encompassing everything from cheap noodle digs to high-end dessert spots. A meal in this city is always memorable.

Noodle Joints

You're never far from a steaming bowl of ramen (wheat), soba (buckwheat), or udon (white wheat) noodles in Tokyo – staples in Japanese cuisine. Slurping is strongly encouraged.

ITASOBA KAORIYA

Map 4; 4-3-10 Ebisu, Shibuya; ///slip.issues.aged; www.foodgate.net/shop/kaoriya

Alive with friendly chatter from its communal tables, this rustic restaurant invites you to settle in and make yourself comfortable. It's a home away from home, where meals are served up on gorgeous wooden trays and pottery dishes. Let the chef know if you want your firm soba noodles thick or thin (they're delicious either way).

MENCHIRASHI

Map 1; 6-13-7 Jingumae, Harajuku; ///balanced.coasted.reveal; www.menchirashi.com

Rub shoulders with Tokyo's cool crowd at this stylish udon joint in Harajuku, Tokyo's mecca of fashion. Unassuming from the outside, inside Menchirashi has the vibe of a retro American diner that's been given a contemporary Japanese twist – think 1950s-style formica tables and walls decorated with tatami mats. Look out for the chefs hand-rolling fresh udon at the front of the shop (your conversations are sure to revolve around their impeccable skill), or, better yet, grab a counter seat to watch all the action up close.

» Don't leave without ordering the unique carbonara-style udon served with a healthy dose of Parmigiano-Reggiano cheese.

GINZA KAGARI

Map 5; 6-4-12 Ginza, Chuo; ///attracts.salutes.ignites; (03) 6263-8900

It'd be easy to miss this diminutive ramen joint, hidden down a back alley in Ginza, were it not for the line of excitable fooodies always congregating outside. Don't let this put you off: it's worth waiting along with them for a bowl of *tori paitan* ramen, the famed house specialty, which uses a rich, creamy, chicken-based broth. Purists may shake their heads at Kagari's modern spin on classic ramen, with non-traditional toppings like avocado and baby corn, but the city's serious noodle slurpers continue to come back here time and again.

Try it!
SOBA FROM SCRATCH

Try your hand at making soba noodles at the Tsukiji Soba Academy (www.soba. specialist.co.jp). Lessons are English-friendly and the soba masters will teach you the tricks of their trade.

Solo, Pair, Crowd

With a noodle joint on pretty much every street in the city, there's always an excuse for a slurp.

FLYING SOLO
Ramen for one
Shibuya's Ramen Nagi makes for a quintessential Japanese ramen experience, with its vending-machine ordering system. If you have a penchant for strong odors, the signature *niboshi* (fish-based ramen) is for you: if not, you've been warned.

IN A PAIR
Date night, sorted
Make it a date at Tokyo Dosanjin in Nakameguro, slurping fine soba paired with sake to match. Be sure to share the *futomaki* sushi rolls as a starter.

FOR A CROWD
Spice up your life
Test your spice limits at Kikanbo in Chiyoda, where you and your friends can choose the level of heat in your bowls of ramen. Add in some extra toppings and get creative with it.

UDON BUZJENBO

Map 4; 1-11-15 Higashiyama, Meguro; ///enable.info.games; www.buzjenbo.tumblr.com

The enjoyment of eating at this cosy udon joint comes from more than just the food. A meal here has the feel of a dinner at a good friend's house, thanks to the affable service and convivial atmosphere. Follow the regulars and order a few sharing plates with your noodles.
» Don't leave without sharing a plate of Udon Buzjenbo's crispy chicken – it's the dish of choice among those in the know.

SARASHINA NUNOYA

Map 5; 1-15-8 Shibadaimon, Minato; ///modules.shells.averages; www.sarashina-nunoya.gorp.jp

From the *noren* (curtains) at the front door to the unfussy Edo-era-inspired interior, the 230-year-old Sarashina Nunoya is an authentic soba store in all respects. It's run by seventh-generation soba maker Eiichi Kaneko, who has an unparalleled passion for *tsuyu* dipping sauce – the staff here learn his unique recipe by taste alone.

T'S TANTAN

Map 5; 1-9-1 Marunouchi, Chiyoda; ///works.groom.recover; www.ts-restaurant.jp/tantan

It's not just commuters passing through Tokyo Station that frequent T's. Veggies and vegans travel across town for this vegan-friendly ramen joint – a rarity in a meat-heavy noodle city – which has gained a cult following for its sesame- and peanut-flavored broths.

Sushi Spots

Eradicating the boundaries of breakfast, lunch, and dinner, sushi is the Japanese delicacy for all seafood cravings at all times. When done right, a flavorsome bite is enough to stop you in your tracks.

SUSHI TOKYO TEN

Map 1; Newoman 2F, 5-24-55 Sendagaya, Shinjuku;
///logged.doted.cloud; www.sushitokyo-ten.com

This intimate restaurant serves only *omakase*, or chef's choice sushi, so you know you're in for a treat. Okay, *omakase* meals aren't exactly synonymous with cheap (prices tend to start at around ¥10,000), but this classy place bucks that trend, delivering a high-quality lunch for a steal at just ¥4,235.

RYU SUSHI

Map 5; 6-6-1 Toyosu, Koto; ///overhead.recover.title; (03) 6633-0053

Sushi doesn't come much fresher – or more authentic – than at this spot in the heart of Toyosu fish market. The chefs here have been making Edo-style sushi for over 50 years (they formerly had a restaurant in Toyosu's predecessor, the now-closed Tsukiji fish market), and draw a steady stream of diners after the early morning tuna

Head up to Toyosu's rooftop terrace to enjoy your sushi with crowd-free views of the Rainbow Bridge.

auction. Don't be surprised if, in true Edo style, the chefs recommend you forego chopsticks and pick up each piece of sushi by hand instead.

UOBEI

Map 1; 2-29-11 Dogenzaka, Shibuya;
///listings.convert.infects; www.genkisushi.co.jp

If there was a mascot for futuristic dining, Uobei would be it. Orders here are placed through the multi-language touch-screen pads in front of each diner, and dishes come zooming out on an electronic track when they're ready. Given its location in party-centric Shibuya, Uobei is unsurprisingly abuzz with a younger crowd come evening, when hungry groups form late-night lines, eager to get the fun started.

GONPACHI NORI-TEMAKI

Map 1; 6-35-3 Jingumae, Harajuku; ///sediment.alarmed.oasis;
www.gonpachi.jp/nori-temaki

Fresh ingredients and an accommodating menu (think vegetarian picks galore) make Gonpachi a winner with health-conscious Tokyoites – they've even got low-carb *temaki* (hand rolls) made with cauliflower rice. Grab one of the counter seats and fill out the step-by-step menu to order, then watch in admiration as the chefs skillfully craft your chosen *temaki* right in front of you.

» **Don't leave without** trying the *natto* (fermented soybean) hand roll – it's a traditional Japanese staple with a ton of health benefits.

KIDOGUCHI

Map 1; 5-6-3 Minamiaoyama, Minato;
///snapper.elite.awkward; (03) 5467-3992

Tucked away in a basement just off the busy streets of Omotesando, this unpretentious sushi joint is the hangout of choice for those who live and work in the area. One of the chefs here spent some time in Canada and can describe each cut of fish in English, so you can have a natter if you're stuck on what to order (or want some company while you wait for your pal to turn up). Note: reserve a table in advance to secure a sought-after spot, especially at lunch, when businessmen and fashionistas spill in for catch-ups and meetings.

TSUJIHAN

Map 5; 3-1-15 Nihonbashi, Chuo; ///elevated.proud.chest;
www.tsujihan-jp.com

With its unassuming front door, you could easily walk past Tsujihan and not realize it's a restaurant. This place is no secret, though: it's Tokyo's king of *kaisendon* (sushi rice bowls), and is famed for its generous dishes piled staggeringly high with portions of freshly chopped seafood. There are just four items on the menu to choose from – basically the same *kaisendon*, but with different quantities of the seafood topping – and each bowl is crafted to order with immaculate precision. Come on a weekday if you can: there are only 12 seats and lines can be long on the weekend.

» Don't leave without finishing off any leftover rice in your bowl with the special broth that's served at the end of the meal. If you need more rice, you can ask for another helping free of charge.

UOGASHI NIHON-ICHI

Map 1; 2-9-1 Dogenzaka, Shibuya; ///this.reframe.lentil;
www.uogashi-nihonichi.imachika.com

What it lacks in seats, Uogashi Nihon-ichi more than makes up for in atmosphere. In the day, this standing sushi bar is the haunt of busy workers, while evening brings young folks and Shibuya locals seeking a quick feed. It's not uncommon to strike up conversation with the affable chef (who knows a bit of English), given the casual, intimate vibe.

KAITENSUSHI GINZA ONODERA

Map 1; 1F, 5-1-6 Jingumae, Shibuya; ///drainage.monopoly.wasp;
www.onodera-group.com/kaitensushi-ginza

Big business in the sushi world, the Ginza Onodera group are behind many *omakase* restaurants across the globe. Yet, the high-quality sushi they're known for came at a hefty price – that is until Kaitensushi opened in 2021. The group's first *kaitenzushi* (conveyor belt sushi) spot has been a hit ever since, letting people try out high-end sushi without an eye-watering bill.

Try it!
SHAPE SOME SUSHI

Sign up for a class with the sociable folk at Cooking Sun Tokyo *(www.cooking-sun.com)*. You'll be taught how to make five types of sushi, as well as miso soup and rolled egg omelette.

Comfort Food

Known as **B-kyu gurume,** *comfort food in Tokyo defines anything that is easy, quick, and resembles home cooking. Cosy joints are built around these beloved dishes: the perfect antidote to long days.*

FUKUHO GYOZA

Map 2; 2-8-6 Shinjuku, Shinjuku; ///whoever.lime.turkey; www.fukuho.net

Any Tokyoite will proudly tell you that their family recipe for gyoza dumplings is the best – but they'll also tell you that this place comes in a (very) close second. Always bustling with Shinjuku's after-work crowds and young diners come evening, this is the kind of spot where catch-ups linger into the early hours and sharing plates of gyoza are devoured (and thus reordered) without a second thought.

BUTAGUMI SHOKUDO

Map 5; Roppongi Hills Metro Hat B2F, 6-4-1 Roppongi, Minato;
///major.flinch.cross; www.butagumi.com/shokudo

There's nothing more comforting on a drizzly weekday evening than settling in at the open-kitchen counter here and letting the scent of *tonkatsu* cooking wash over you. A beloved Japanese staple, *tonkatsu* consists of panko-crusted deep-fried pork cutlets, served with bottomless rice, shredded cabbage salad, miso soup, and pickles. This laid-back spot happens to be the casual version of Butagumi's more upscale *tonkatsu* restaurant, so you can enjoy the same quality meal for a fraction of the cost – and without the crowds.

MONJA KURA

Map 5; 3-9-9 Tsukishima, Chuo; ///rocky.message.greeting;
www.monja-kura.gorp.jp

It says a lot about this place that, in an area saturated with around 80 *monjayaki* restaurants (Tokyo's own version of *okonomiyaki*), waiting in line doesn't deter even the hungriest of people. That's all down to its simplicity: settle on *teppanyaki* tables, order the mixture by the bowl, and cook on the hotplate (ask for help if you're a first-timer). It's a no-frills spot that lets the beloved pan-fried batter dish do the talking.

ONIGIRI BONGO

Map 3; 2-26-3 Kitaotsuka, Toshima; ///reviewed.lights.rosette;
www.onigiribongo.info

When Tokyoites need a quick snack on-the-go, the *onigiri* rice ball is the first port of call – a staple on the shelves of every convenience store. In fact, it's so good that Yumiko Ukon decided to turn the humble snack into a full-on meal at Onigiri Bongo. If there was a spot to overrule the supermarket, it's this one, where Yumiko makes over half a million balls in a single year for regulars who can't get enough.

» Don't leave without sizing up your stuffed rice ball with another filling for an extra ¥50. Ask Yumiko for her recommendations.

Solo, Pair, Crowd

Comfort food is exactly that in Tokyo: comforting, familiar, and hopelessly satisfying at all times.

FLYING SOLO
Healthy retreat
For a vegetarian meal that doesn't compromise on flavor, stop by the intimate space at Alaska Zwei in Meguro for brown rice plates, colorful salads, and Japanese-style curry.

IN A PAIR
Sharing is caring
Oden is the ultimate Japanese comfort food, consisting of veggies, chicken, and fish cakes simmered in a flavorful broth. It's best shared at Samon, a specialist under the train tracks near Nakameguro Station.

FOR A CROWD
Chefs at work
Gather your friends for a round of *okonomiyaki* at Hiroki, where the savory pancakes are cooked right in front of you on the open *teppanyaki* grill. Who needs to go to the theater with a show like this?

GYUKATSU MOTOMURA

Map 1; B1F, 2-19-17 Shibuya, Shibuya; ///pity.sizes.together;
www.gyukatsu-motomura.com

Tokyoites will tell you that this is one of the best spots to enjoy Japan's famed wagyu beef, and who's to argue? The line outside certainly never does. Once you're inside (likely after an hour of waiting), you can cook your beef cutlet to tender perfection on a stone grill.

KITCHEN PUNCH

Map 4; 2-7-10 Kamimeguro, Meguro; ///audibly.vanilla.bunch;
(03) 3712-1084

Serving up inexpensive, hearty dishes in homey surrounds, *shokudo* (casual restaurants or cafeterias) epitomize comfort in Japan. Kitchen Punch is one of the best, and has been keeping Nakameguro regulars happy since 1966. Come for the omurice (omelette over rice), a popular Western-influenced Japanese dish.

SUPERIORITY BURGER

Map 4; 5-33-7 Setagaya, Shibuya; ///going.flagged.burst; (03) 6432-9360

This vegan burger joint might be an import from NYC, but as befits this unique city, Tokyo's spun it as its own. You'll still find American classics on the menu, but it's the exclusive Japanese burgers – made with locally sourced ingredients like sesame yuba and marinated tofu – that really shine. It's fast food that's superior in name and taste.

» Don't leave without rounding off your meal with homemade vegan gelato, of which there are three seasonal flavors to choose from.

Special Occasion

*Though home to some of the most revered restaurants
in the world (you'll lose count of the Michelin stars),
Tokyo's most special spots are not all fine dining and
expense. Celebrate your way, on your budget.*

SIO

**Map 2; 1-35-3 Uehara, Shibuya; ///written.tune.division;
www.sio-yoyogiuehara.com**

Local foodies eagerly await their birthdays for an excuse to splash
out here. A laid-back yet refined bistro, Sio earned itself a Michelin
star in 2019 for its innovative fusion of *washoku* (Japanese cuisine)
and French fare. Watching renowned chef Shusaku Toba cook up
a storm in the open kitchen is the icing on the (birthday) cake.

ISE SUEYOSHI

**Map 5; 4-2-15 Nishiazabu, Minato, Hiroo;
///fried.deduced.blanket; www.isesueyoshi.blog.fc2.com**

Locals rave about this spot so much that out-of-towners make it their
mission to bag a table whenever they visit Tokyo. They all come for
kaiseki – a traditional multicourse meal that brings the best of
Japanese seasonal produce straight to your plate. Thoughtfully

selected ingredients (mainly sourced from the Japanese city of Ise), beautifully presented food, and friendly staff make a visit here one to brag about when you get home.

≫ Don't leave without striking up a chat with chef Yuki Tanaka, who enjoys explaining the backstory behind his dishes.

TOKYO SHIBA TOFUYA UKAI

Map 5; 4-4-13 Shibakoen, Minato; ///movies.reshape.pothole; www.ukai.co.jp

Nothing says special like entering another world – and that's exactly what happens at this Edo-era-esque restaurant, which stands in the shadow of Tokyo Tower. Kimono-clad staff greet you in the garden before leading you into one of the dining rooms – all set up inside a samurai-era merchant's house – where tofu dishes are elegantly served. It's a quintessential Japanese dining experience that's guaranteed to take you back in time.

Shh!

Amour Tokyo (*www.amour tokyojapan.com*) is the kind of spot visitors overlook, mistaking it for a private home. But this place is anything but. Inside, seasonal produce from Japan is prepared using French cooking techniques, creating flavorful dinner courses that merge the two cultures seamlessly. There are only five tables available, so book ahead for a perfectly intimate, one-of-a-kind celebration.

YAKITORI IMAI

Map 2; 3-42-11 Jingumae, Shibuya, Aoyama;
///nappy.ambition.teaching; www.yakitoriimai.jp

Simple yakitori grilled chicken skewers, classic Japanese soul food
that's often eaten cheap and quick, are taken to new heights at this
smart restaurant. You know you're in for a treat when the chef takes
note of each diner and seasons the chicken to the customer's taste.
And you know you're in for an even bigger treat when there's a
well-curated selection of wine awaiting a yakitori pairing.

BON

Map 3; 1-2-11 Ryusen, Taito; ///rise.merchant.drilled; www.fuchabon.co.jp

Bon specializes in *shojin ryori*, the vegetarian cuisine eaten by Zen
Buddhist monks in Japan. Everything is taken care of with such
elegant simplicity, from the tranquil, sprawling garden to the
delicately presented works of edible art. Truly, less is more here.

FLORILÈGE

Map 2; B1F, 2-5-4 Jingumae, Shibuya;
///swelling.racing.dumpy; www.aoyama-florilege.jp

Proud recipient of not one but two Michelin stars, this sultry spot is
renowned for wowing locals with imaginative and sustainable French
cuisine. In fact, the friendly, open-kitchen concept was created to
encourage diners and chefs to exchange conversation with each
course, letting guests learn more about the food and the detail that
goes into each dish. (As you can imagine, local food writers and

Check Florilège's social pages to see when *kakigori* (shaved ice dessert) events are held during the year.

cuisine connoisseurs adore Florilège.) You'll have to be speedy about making a reservation for lunch or dinner, as they can disappear in a flash – it's that good.

LOCALE

Map 4; 1-17-22 Meguro, Meguro; ///bounty.tools.vented; www.locale.tokyo

Warmth emanates from every corner of this farm-to-table spot. Chef Katy Cole greets every guest like a life-long friend, working her magic in the open kitchen while you settle at a rustic wooden table. Order the tasting menu (which changes according to the seasons), and the food will come artfully served on gorgeous tableware handcrafted by Katy herself. What follows will be a gloriously intimate evening, where glasses of red wine are clinked and joyous conversations had.

TEMPURA ABE

Map 5; Subaru Bldg B1F, 4-3-7 Ginza, Chuo; ///inhales.kipper.rocky; www.tempura-abe-ginza.gorp.jp

In a city where tempura – a deep-fried, beloved Japanese dish – is associated with casual dining, it's a hard task finding a special-occasion-worthy spot to enjoy it in. That's where this old family favorite comes in. Abe, the chef here, has over 30 years' experience in this dish, and watching him prepare his top-notch tempura (some would say the capital's best) from a counter seat is unforgettable.

» Don't leave without ordering the *kakiage tendon* at lunch. It features a crisp tempura fritter topped with a tempura egg yolk.

Beloved Bakeries

Tokyo could easily rival Paris with its abundance of homely bakeries. Japan has something of a newfound love affair with bread, so join the locals and pick up a freshly baked loaf from a neighborhood bakery.

VANER

Map 3; 2-15-6 Uenosakuragi, Taito;
///evenings.method.lectures; (03) 5834-8137

Nestled inside an Edo-era home, Vaner may look like just another Japanese bakery from the outside. But inside, the Scandinavian open kitchen aesthetic hints at something unique. After honing his craft in Norway, owner Miyawaki-san decided to revitalize the Tokyo bakery scene by merging these two cultures. Expect a mix of Japanese wheat and Norwegian grains in every sourdough loaf and earthy croissant.

LEVAIN

Map 2; 2-43-13 Tomigaya, Shibuya; ///orchestra.rejected.scary;
(03) 3468-9669

Shibuya residents only have one place in mind come morning: Levain. They all come to collect wild yeast-leavened bread, either ordering by the number of slices for their lunchtime sandwiches or purchasing a full

For more Levain treats, stop by the adjoining café, Le Chalet, for pretty plates of fresh salads and warming soups.

loaf to tide them over for a few days. It's the kind of bakery that wouldn't be out of place in the French countryside, complete with rustic, time-worn decor.

UNIVERSAL BAKES AND CAFE

Map 4; 5-9-1 Daita, Setagaya; ///gears.scramble.prices; (03) 6335-4972

It's rare to come across a 100 percent vegan bakery anywhere in the world, let alone Tokyo, where plant-based dining isn't yet on the rise. Enter Universal Bakes and Cafe. Here, you'll find the usual bakery suspects, but with a twist: apple-flavored French toast, crispy rolls filled with *amazake* (a fermented sweet rice drink), caramel bread, whole-wheat croissants. Given that every baked good fools your tastebuds in the absence of butter, eggs, and milk, it's no surprise that non-vegans are tempted to travel across town for a taste.

PATH

Map 2; 1-44-2 Tomigaya, Shibuya; ///sizing.posed.copy; (03) 6407-0011

Looking for a Tokyo take on brunch? There's hardly a better place than Path. This bistro has a fiercely loyal fanbase among its devoted Shibuya locals, who form ever-lively lines outside whatever the weather. Once seated, they all seem to order the same dish: the signature Dutch pancakes, served with slices of prosciutto and a ball of burrata cheese. Why not follow their lead?

» Don't leave without buying one of the buttery chocolate croissants to enjoy while walking through nearby Yoyogi Park.

Solo, Pair, Crowd

After a quick bite? In need of a hearty breakfast? There's always a time and place for a baked treat in Tokyo.

FLYING SOLO
A river accompaniment

Pick up freshly baked goods – made from organic ingredients – from Lotus Baguette before taking a leisurely walk down the Meguro River.

IN A PAIR
Brunch for two

Plan a BFF catch-up at Criss Cross in Omotesando on the weekend. You can dine on French toast and pancakes in a relaxing space.

IN A CROWD
Muffins with mates

Pile in on the large communal tables at the Aussie-Japanese café Cibi, a cool warehouse-like space in Yanaka. A freshly baked muffin is the perfect treat alongside a flat white.

TOLO PAN TOKYO

Map 4; 3-14-3 Higashiyama, Meguro;
///websites.photos.filer; www.tolotokyo.com

A community feel defines this nifty little bakery. No matter how busy it gets (and it gets busy), flour-smattered bakers always greet you with a warm welcome. Customers squeeze in, awaiting the fresh croissants that emerge from the kitchen and disappear into bags quicker than the chef can bake a new batch. It's takeaway only; fortunately, the neighborhood makes for a charming bread-fueled stroll.

BRICOLAGE BREAD & CO

Map 5; 6-15-1 Roppongi, Minato; ///ports.declares.legend;
www.bricolagebread.com

This place bakes wildly original breads, with dough infused with everything from toasted green tea to red bean paste. Most popular is the signature Bricolage bread – made with heirloom grains with a caramelized crust, and best enjoyed as an open-faced sandwich.

» Don't leave without ordering a coffee, the beans of which are provided by beloved local roasters Fuglen, for a serious caffeine kick.

VIRON

Map 1; 33-8 Udagawacho, Shibuya; ///prefer.line.hairpin; (03) 5458-1770

There's an air of Paris in this boulangerie, where French pastries, European-style bread, and thick-cut rustic sandwiches are served up to chic regulars. It's a grab-and-go affair, so take your goods to the rooftop of the adjacent Tokyu Department Store and enjoy in the sun.

Sweet Treats

Tokyo sure has a sweet tooth. Dessert culture is a big deal here, where tucking into a donut after breakfast, a traditional sweet with a cup of tea, and an artfully crafted parfait before bedtime is the norm.

TAIYAKI HIIRAGI

Map 4; 1-3-1 Ebisu, Shibuya; ///domestic.films.puff; (03) 3473-7050

This Tokyo institution has been turning out traditional Japanese *taiyaki* (fish-shaped pastries filled with *anko*, a sweet red bean paste) for over a decade, making it a no-brainer for a post-lunch pick-me-up. A takeaway-only shop, it sometimes accumulates a line – but don't worry, it moves fast, since folks are eager to sink their teeth into these nostalgic treats.

PARFAITERIA BEL

Map 1; Shindaimune Social Bldg 3F, 1-7-10 Dogenzaka, Shibuya; ///capers.puts.respond; www.risotteria-gaku.net

In a city filled with late-night dive bars, this evening-only dessert café is a welcome retreat for those who prefer indulgent sweet treats to a well-shaken cocktail. Young couples and groups of girlfriends linger over the show-stopping parfaits: fashioned from

Pair your creamy parfait with a coffee – you may need the caffeine if you stay here until 1am close.

handmade ingredients and topped with everything from mini macarons to fresh fruit, these gravity-defying desserts are almost too pretty to eat. (Almost.)

HARITTS DONUTS & COFFEE

Map 2; 1-34-2 Uehara, Shibuya; ///market.holiday.plenty; www.haritts.com

It's not hard to find a donut in Tokyo, whether prepackaged in convenience stores or sitting on bakery shelves all day. But what is hard is finding a donut of high quality: fresh, fluffy, and not oily. That's where Haritts comes in. There's something incredibly exclusive about nabbing a donut here: every ball is handmade and takes a laborious two hours to make, which means they only sell a limited number a day. To top it off, there's a rotating menu of limited-edition flavors.

» Don't leave without trying the shop's own blend of aromatic coffee – it's the perfect accompaniment to a sugar-dusted donut.

HIMITSUDO

Map 3; 3-11-18 Yanaka, Taito; ///fruity.toolbar.topped;
www.himitsudo.com

Kakigori (shaved iced) is traditionally a summer treat in Japan, but its popularity has seen dedicated shops serve it up year-round. Ask any local where to get your fix and they'll direct you to Himitsudo – and tell you that it's known as the "long-lined" shop. Once you get your towering bowl of fluffy ice – shaved by hand and drizzled with seasonal fresh fruit purees – you'll be glad you waited for an hour.

TOSHI YOROIZUKA

Map 5; Tokyo Midtown East, 9-7-2 Akasaka, Minato;
///lashed.stripped.belonging; www.grand-patissier.info

After a dessert with a fine-dining spin? This place is as much about
the show as it is the menu. Whipped up right in front of your eyes
by skilled pastry chefs, the delectable desserts look more like works
of art than tasty sweets. It's the sweet-treat equivalent of watching a
sushi chef craft his specials: head to the counter for a front row seat.
» Don't leave without trying a seasonal dessert – chestnut-inspired
treats in the fall and cherry-blossom flavors in spring.

BAKE CHEESE TART

Map 2; Lumine EST Shinjuku 3-38-1, Shinjuku; ///middle.qualify.early;
www.cheesetart.com

Hailing from the island of Hokkaido, the nation's dairy prefecture,
Bake is the brand responsible for kicking off the cheese-tart craze
in mainland Japan. Crispy, buttery pastry on the outside, warm
gooey cheesecake-like center: the cheese tart here is the ultimate
luxe treat. Picking up a six-pack box for a dinner party gift or as a
feast for the office always goes down well.

SUZUKIEN ASAKUSA

Map 3; 3-4-3 Asakusa, Taito; ///acid.snatched.level; www.suzukien.tokyo

Matcha tea is the taste that defines Japan – so beloved, in fact,
that they've even made an ice cream out of it. Suzukien Asakusa
takes the craze to a whole new level, stocking what they label as the

world's richest matcha-flavored gelato. In the same way that you brew a cup of tea to your preferred strength, you order your ice cream by intensity level here (and you're bound to run into extreme fans who opt for the highest – level seven). So, on a scale of one to seven, how much do you love matcha?

FRUITS AND SEASON

Map 4; Green Palace 1F, 1-10-1 Ebisu Nishi, Shibuya;
///alas.includes.intro; www.fruitsandseason.com

Anyone familiar with Japanese snacks will know about the luxurious fruit sando – fresh fruit sandwiched between *shokupan* (Japanese milk bread) and whipped cream. It's been a go-to treat for over a century in Japan, but fruits and season took it to a whole new level when it opened the first vegan fruit sando joint in 2021. Here, egg- and dairy-free *shokupan* are filled with soy-based cream and seasonal fruit like kiwi, strawberry, and mango. Word to the wise: pictures of the pretty treat tend to go viral, so join the queues early for a snap and a snack before they sell out.

Try it!
TEATIME TREATS

Learn how to make dainty teatime sweets by signing up for a *wagashi*-making workshop at the Simply Oishii Japanese Cooking Class & Wagashi School *(www.simplyoishii.com)*.

A morning of
Tokyo's classic food

Hibiya Park

There are many things that instantly define Tokyo's food scene: the cheap charms of *konbini* (convenience stores), more Michelin stars than any other city on the planet, delicate teatime sweets, wonderfully inventive vending machine restaurants. It's not just about the food on your plate (though a serving of ramen or sushi is heavenly), but the culture that's embedded in buying, making, and eating that food. There's no better way to start the day than dipping into time-honored haunts and learning the art behind quintessential Tokyo treats.

NISHI-SHINBASHI

SHINBASHI

1. Lawson
2-15-13 Tsukiji, Chuo
///walnuts.chose.roaring

2. Tsukiji Outer Market
Around 4-16-16 Tsukiji, Chuo;
www.tsukiji.or.jp
///mason.almost.comment

3. Ginza Fugetsudo
6-6-1 Ginza, Chuo;
www.ginza-fugetsudo.co.jp
///training.quit.hobbit

4. Ginza Mitsukoshi
4-6-16 Ginza, Chuo;
www.mitsukoshi.mistore.
jp/ginza
///gone.fixtures.advising

Sukiyabashi Jiro
///drainage.dashes.unity

Namiyoke Inari Shrine
///slope.freshen.windows

Known as the "world's best sushi restaurant," **Sukiyabashi Jiro** in Ginza really put fine-dining sushi on the map in Tokyo.

SOTOBORI - DORI

NAMIKI - DORI

GINZA

Lunch at
GINZA MITSUKOSHI

A *depachika* (basement food hall in a department store) is as classic as a bento box in Tokyo. Combine the two and pick up a box here, then head to the rooftop to enjoy it with a view.

③

CHUO - DORI

④

Get artistic at
GINZA FUGETSUDO

Learn the art of *wagashi* at a hands-on workshop here. The flavors of these traditional Japanese sweets, filled with fruit or beans, change with the seasons. Pair your creation with tea.

GINZA

SHOWA - DORI

DORI

HARUMI - DORI

MIYUKI - DORI

Fuel up at
LAWSON

Pick up Tokyo's most loved snack, an *onigiri* rice ball, from this convenience store chain to start your day.

①

CHUO - ICHIBA - DORI

SHIN - OHASHI DORI

TSUKIJI

HARUMI - DORI

Mooch around
TSUKIJI OUTER MARKET

Soak up the vibrant atmosphere of this iconic market, where locals tuck into sushi for breakfast and vendors sell tempting street food.

②

NAMIYOKE - DORI

HIGASHI-
SHINBASHI

Memorial stones found at **Namiyoke Inari Shrine** – often dubbed the "sushi shrine" – are dedicated to the fish used in Tokyo's seafood.

Hama Rikyu Garden

0 meters		300
0 yards		300

DRINK

Drinks are more than just thirst quenchers in Tokyo. Cocktails are an expression of artistry, tea clears the mind at elaborate ceremonies, and sake marks special occasions.

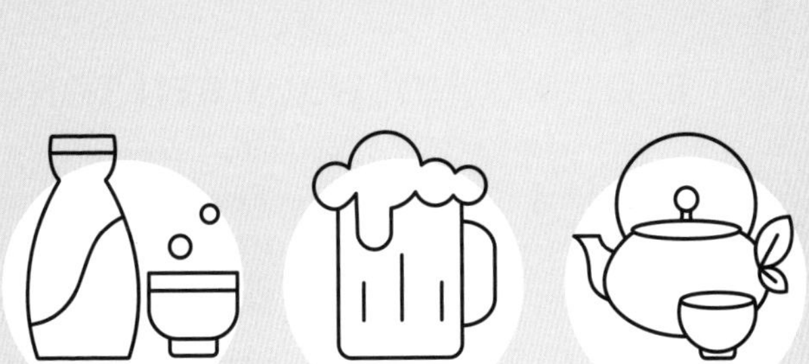

Cocktail Joints

Trust Tokyo to turn the process of making a cocktail into an art form. World-class bartenders are seriously dedicated to their craft – visiting these bars is as much for the mixology show as it is to enjoy a tipple.

BAR TRENCH

Map 4; 1-5-8 Ebisunishi, Shibuya; ///raged.flow.leafing; www.small-axe.net/bar-trench

Everything about this suave speakeasy evokes the prohibition era. Tucked away in the backstreets of Ebisu, this is where those in-the-know come for original concoctions served up by dapper bartenders. It's the spot of choice for those looking to lay low for a relaxed evening (made all the harder when the absinthe comes out).

BLOODY ANGLE DOUGEN TONG

Map 1; B1F, 2-15-1 Dogenzaka, Shibuya; ///strictly.noble.meaning; www.bloodyangle.tokyo

Daytime coffees turn into evening cocktails once 8pm hits at this mellow spot – a fashionable café by day and a neon-illuminated bar by night. Founded by local legend MC/producer Ryuzo, Bloody Angle blurs the lines between record bar and classic Japanese *kissaten* (coffee shops inspired by tearooms). It's popular with after-work crowds, who settle into the booths, sip an old-fashioned, and enjoy the expansive soundtrack.

MIXOLOGY SALON

Map 5; Ginza Six 13F, 6-10-1 Ginza, Chuo;
///debater.handed.batches; www.ginza6.tokyo

Shoppers always make time for a pitstop at this classy bar, located on the 13th floor of the Ginza Six shopping center. You'd be forgiven for thinking it's your average tearoom when you walk in, and that's kind of the point. Nothing typifies Japan more than tea, and this calming space lets you indulge in expertly crafted "teatails", made using various leaves to create infused spirits.

» Don't leave without trying the signature matcha old-fashioned, topped with delicate flakes of gold leaf. It's luxury in a glass.

Shh!

With a nondescript exterior, no signage, and a limited menu (plus, frankly, an uninviting name), Bar Toilet in Shinjuku is an anti-bar in almost all regards, but that's why it's so special. The low-lit space fits about six people by the counter, four in the corner, and an empty bathtub that takes up 50 percent of the venue's occupancy. The bar makes its fruit liqueur in big glass jars on the counter — you can choose between the latest homemade *yuzu* and *umeshu* brews.

BAR ISHINOHANA

Map 1; 3-6-2 Shibuya, Shibuya; ///royally.nickname.shopping;
www.ishinohana.com

Fine craftsmanship and creativity define this classy bar, where founder Shinobu Ishigaki whips up some of the best fruit- and vegetable-based cocktails in the city. It's a sacred affair, where well-dressed couples whisper in hushed tones while Ishigaki makes fruity gin and tonics in silence at the bar. As expected, the menu changes with the seasons, giving you an excuse to return multiple times a year.

GRANDFATHER'S

Map 1; B1F, 1-24-7 Shibuya, Shibuya; ///steers.riots.clearly;
www.grandfather.jp/shibuya

Hidden down a narrow set of stairs, this unassuming bar feels as cosy as your grandfather's actual house, with a dark wooden interior and record-lined walls oozing retro-Tokyo vibes. A smooth crackle of music plays through the speakers from the DJ, who mixes a soundtrack as carefully as the bartender whips up a great highball.

THE SG CLUB

Map 1; 1-7-8 Jinnan, Shibuya; ///releases.spots.snapped;
www.sg-management.jp

Split into two floors and, well, essentially two bars, the SG Club is all about letting patrons seek out the area that suits their mood best. The first floor, known as Guzzle, drums up a sociable vibe, where espresso martinis are drunk in quick succession. Sip, in the basement, is a more elegant and intimate affair, with drinkers lingering over complex cocktails (heck, you can even get your shoes shined). So, what's your vibe: a casual drinking den or a stylish speakeasy?

BAR OAK

Map 5; Tokyo Station Hotel 2F, 1-9-1 Marunouchi, Chiyoda;
///flats.renders.eggs; www.tokyostationhotel.jp

Hotel bars aren't usually something to brag about, but this one stands out from the rest. That's all down to Hisashi Sugimoto, the bartender who's been at its helm since the 1950s. Settle in on a counter stall in the luxurious space and you'll get a front-row seat to Sugimoto shaking up a signature cocktail, which is reason enough to visit.

» Don't leave without ambling through the adjoining Tokyo Station – the busiest station in Tokyo and a magnificent work of architecture. Expect to find restaurants and even an art gallery.

AOYAMA TUNNEL

Map 1; 4-5-9 Shibuya, Shibuya; ///magpie.saloons.crunch;
www.aoyama-tunnel.com

This cool bar is the failsafe place where young creatives go to drink affordable classic cocktails when everything else is shutting down. With its edgy location (in an underpass, hence the name), chandelier-lined ceiling, moody red-lit interior, and mismatched seating, it sits somewhere between kitsch and nonchalantly shabby. There's a house-party vibe to it all, complete with a DJ spinning low-key techno music until dawn.

Breweries and Beer Bars

Sipping on a crisp lager after a long day is a much-loved pastime in the city. The beer scene has always been flooded by big players, but craft beer is seeing a boom, too, with brewers concocting unique blends.

JOLLY'S

Map 4; 3-15-12 Higashi, Shibuya; ///staple.tablets.brass;
www.jollys.jp

This isn't your regular liquor store. Sure, you can pick up cans of craft beer to enjoy in the comfort of your own home, but local office workers choose to knock them back in this Americana-inspired,

Try it!
BREW A BEER

Dive a little deeper into the local craft beer scene by creating your own recipe at Hitachino Brewing Lab *(www.hitachino.cc/brewing-lab)*. You'll learn how to brew from scratch with world-renowned brewers.

standing-only space after a long day. Between munching on hot dogs and scouting the colorful, well-stocked fridges for the next brew to try, patrons can listen to the faint sounds of bands rehearsing in the studio behind the bar. It's the epitome of cool.

T.Y. HARBOR BREWERY

Map 5; 2-1-3 Higashishinagawa, Shinagawa;
///scarcely.homework.purely; www.tysons.jp/tyharbor

One of the very few places in the city where you can drink canalside, this hip brewpub wins the award for best views. Despite the former warehouse origins, it's a fancy (but not too fancy) spot where friends head for a high-quality dinner and brew. On good-weather days, you'll be waiting with the rest of the city for a waterfront terrace table, but killer views of Tennozu Isle while you sip on a crisp pale ale and tuck into a heavenly pizza are your reward.

» Don't leave without ordering the Amber Sandy Gaff, a craft beer cocktail mix of sweet amber ale and ginger ale.

YONA YONA BEER WORKS

Map 2; B1F, 3-18-20, Minato, Minamiaoyama;
///ocean.balance.feel; www.yonayonabeerworks.com

Spend enough time trawling convenience store fridges and you'll spot the oh-so-popular Yona Yona beers taking up prime real estate on the shelves. Staunch fans swerve these bottled brews in favor of this tap room, where fresh variations of the ubiquitious beer – made by Yo-Ho Brewing – are served with light dinner options.

Solo, Pair, Crowd

In a city this passionate about beer, you're never far from a bar that serves up the good stuff.

FLYING SOLO
Beer to go
Drinking in public is perfectly legal in Tokyo – and encouraged at Shimokitazawa's Tap and Growler, where you can buy fresh craft brews on tap by the reusable growler.

IN A PAIR
Happy and you know it
Plan a catch-up at Shinjuku's Vector Beer Factory, one of the inner city's most well-stocked and cheapest beer bars, where tap beers are happy-hour prices all day long.

FOR A CROWD
Party all night
The stylishly minimal Norwegian bar O/L in Shibuya regularly hosts DJ sets on Fridays and weekends, making it a buzzing destination for partying with a refreshing Nordic beer (or two).

TWO FINGERS

Map 6; 3-54-2, Toshima, Ikebukuro; ///brave.odds.working;
www.twofingers-craftbeer.com

Run by a Japanese-Australian couple who met through a beer-loving social network group, this no-frills bar lets the beer do the talking. It's become a word-of-mouth victory, where regulars bring new faces who share a passion for local brews, all of which rotate on tap here.

Y.Y.G. BREWERY & BEER KITCHEN

Map 2; Ohchu Daiichi Bldg 1F & 7F, 2-18-3 Yoyogi, Shibuya;
///jeering.things.gross; www.yygbrewery.com

There's an inner-city residential vibe to this brewpub, populated by cool locals indulging in a wind-down drink. When these regulars get peckish, they fill out the seventh floor "beer kitchen", where the same beer selection as downstairs is enjoyed alongside an "American French" menu (think truffle salt fries and mini-oyster burgers).

SPRING VALLEY BREWERY

Map 4; Log Road Daikanyama, 13-1 Daikanyamacho, Shibuya;
///civic.gets.gearbox; www.springvalleybrewery.jp

One of major beer brand Kirin's forays into the craft beer world, this slick, modern brewery serves over 20 types of artisan beers – some even made on-site. It's an open, relaxed space where creatives spend leisurely afternoons drinking on the sun-soaked tables.

» Don't leave without ordering the unusual Jazzberry beer, infused with raspberry and made fresh with wine yeast.

Wine Bars

There's been something of a wine renaissance of late, with niche natural wines and domestic varieties taking pride of place in tiny bars. Passionate sommeliers love nothing more than guiding budding oenophiles.

LUG

Map 2; 2-19-1 Hatagaya, Shibuya; ///elevate.factor.hoaxes; www.lug-hatagaya.com

A rustically furnished café by day, Lug truly shines after dark, when cups of coffee are swapped out for glasses of natural wine (that's wine made with minimal intervention on a small scale). Drawing in regulars is the resident sommelier Honzawa-san, more affectionately known as "Pon-chan" to the locals. A living encyclopedia on all things natural wine, she'll guide you through the 100-plus bottle selection with ease.

HAGARE

Map 4; 2-9-3 Kitazawa, Setagaya; ///helping.channel.dating; www.kaldi.co.jp/cafe/hagare_shimokita

Loosely translating to "come off" in Japanese, Hagare sums up this restaurant's sustainable ethos of offering wine in bottles that may have detached or less-than-perfect labels, but are still perfectly

Continue your night with live music at nearby Club Que, where local bands and DJs perform.

drinkable. Because of this, wines here are reasonably priced, and you can easily share a few bottles alongside some dishes from the Italian-inspired menu.

SHUBIDUBA

Map 5; 4-14-18 Tsukiji, Chuo; ///honest.dweller.seat;
www.shubiduba-tsukiji.com

You'd be forgiven for walking straight past this bar. Nestled in Tsukiji outer market, with an unassuming facade that blends in with the neighboring shops, it's something of a secret. In-the-know shoppers find respite from the bustle in this standing-only spot, sipping on a glass of Japanese or international vino. There's at least 250 different varieties, so popping back on every market visit is a given.

» **Don't leave without** trying a glass of hot sake. If you're visiting during the cooler months, it's a great way to warm up.

AHIRU STORE

Map 2; 1-19-4 Tomigaya, Shibuya; ///parting.hobbies.demand;
(03) 5454-2146

This tiny haunt in trendy Tomigaya has a big reputation. You'll know you've arrived when you see dedicated folks lining up (hours before it opens at 6pm), hoping to grab one of the sought-after eight seats at the bar. It's a spot of pilgrimage for natural wine fanatics, who come for the well-curated selection of bottles mainly sourced from France, all of which are pretty impossible to find elsewhere in the city.

WINESTAND WALTZ

Map 4; 4-24-3 Ebisu, Shibuya; ///deed.successes.manuals

This tiny standing-only bar fits about ten people, but that's part of its charm. Despite lacking a website or landline, it's built up a firm following through word-of-mouth, thanks to the excellent selection of international wines and the expert advice of friendly owner Yasuhiro Ooyama. It's clear he has a passion for European tastes, stocking the bar with Baccarat glasses and retro French posters, but ask him what to drink and chances are he'll suggest a Japanese drop.

SANSAN

Map 2; 1-2-1 Uehara, Shibuya; ///young.voters.starch;
(03) 6407-0333

It makes sense that Sansan means "bright" in Japanese, given the sunny demeanor of this inviting wine bar. Sure, it's well lit and flanked in light timber, but the warmth primarily comes from owner Yuko Enomoto, who founded this bar as a place for weary workers to drop by for a casual drink on the way home. Get chatting to her and she'll advise you on what to order (it's usually her current favorite).

SANITA

Map 2; 2-27-4 Nishihara, Shibuya; ///moved.gourmet.contexts;
www.sanitatokyo.com

This Brooklyn-inspired spot has all the things you want from a great neighborhood bar: a carefully curated playlist, owners as friendly as the regulars, and natural wine in artistic bottles that you'll be itching to take home and display. The atmosphere is as chilled out as it gets, too – particularly on a warm night, when friends lounge against the open-brick storefront with glasses of orange wine.

» **Don't leave without** also trying a New York style classic cocktail, served with southern Italian small plates.

DRINK & MOOD MOU
Map 4; 3F-A, 2-32-7 Kitazawa, Setagaya;
///machinery.posed.cheeses; (03) 6874-1957

Nothing says hipster like walls lined with street-art-style images, plants hanging from the ceiling, and DJ decks set up in the corner. With only two tables and two benches to perch on, Mou isn't the kind of place you settle for the whole evening. Rather, those donning the latest street-style garms rock up to either start or end their night, chatting away with a glass of natural wine while tunes play out.

Well hidden in the backstreets of Kiyosumi-Shirakawa and accessed through a nondescript building, Fujimaru Winery *(2-5-3 Miyoshi, Koto)* is the epitome of an off-the-beaten-track bar. This riverside wine cellar labels itself as an urban winery, where the house wines on the menu – red, white, rosé, and sparkling – are all brewed on-site. It's easy to while away the hours here, sipping on a glass, nibbling some cheese bites, and gazing out toward the picturesque river.

Sake, Shochu, and Whisky Spots

When it comes to liquor, Tokyo is a prolific producer.
Sip on home-grown spirits like sake or shochu,
or savor a glass of whisky, internationally
imported and given the Tokyo-spin.

HASEGAWA SAKETEN

Map 5; 2-1-1 Nihonbashihoncho, Chuo; ///hits.clash.limped; www.hasegawasaketen.com

On the surface, this sleek spot is a classy liquor store, but cross the threshold and you'll find a luxe little sake bar around the corner. While those seeking a night at home trawl the well-stocked refrigerators, a well-dressed crowd settle in on bar stools for a pre-dinner tipple.

WAKAZE TOKYO

Map 4; 1-15-12 Taishido, Setagaya; ///amended.merchant.locked; www.wakaze-store.com

Sake might be 2,000 years old, but the guys behind this *sakagura* (sake brewery) have their sights set on the future. They experiment with brewing techniques near-daily, challenging the possibilities of

Reserve a spot for the monthly tasting menu, where seasonal dishes are paired with new sake brews. sake and creating new recipes. The fruits of their labor are served up in a fittingly cutting-edge space, kitted out with tanks and a compressor used to make sake.

WHISKY LIBRARY

Map 1; 2F, 5-5-24 Minamiaoyama, Minato;
///genetics.udder.taxi; www.tokyo-whisky-library.com

There's a secret-society feel to this plush bar, hidden inside the Santa Chiara Church complex and surrounded by bookcases that lead into the "library." But it's not just for whisky connoisseurs. Stocking more than 1,000 distilled spirits from Japan and around the world, it prides itself on being a space where you can learn more about these fine malts (it calls itself a library, after all). It's a rare find: a whisky bar that oozes sophistication and charisma without being intimidating.

» Don't leave without ordering the Comfortable Hot Fashioned, a warm spin on an old-fashioned cocktail featuring Japanese green tea.

MEISHU CENTER

Map 3; Lions Plaza Ochanomizu 1F, 1-2-12 Yushima, Bunkyo;
///reddish.loafer.treating; www.nihonshu.com

A delightful simplicity defines the proceedings here, where getting tipsy goes hand-in-hand with a bit of sake education. The staff (and the odd friendly regular) help you navigate the museum-like fridges with their knowledge of flavors and ingredients. It's far from luxurious, but the wide selection and affordable prices can't be beaten.

Liked by the locals

"Himekura's owner-chef Mr. Tsuchiyama is a true shochu savant. He's friends with many experts and attends major tasting events in Tokyo. He's an excellent shochu resource and a good cook to boot!"

CHRISTOPHER PELLEGRINI, SHOCHU EXPERT

HIMEKURA

Map 6; 4-26-6 Mukojima, Sumida;
///trickle.pushy.builder; (03) 3625-1856

This is a real hole-in-the-wall spot. In fact, the owner, Mr. Tsuchiyama, literally blew a hole in the wall of his establishment so his guests could get a good view of nearby Tokyo Skytree while they drink. It's this kind of dedication to his customers and shochu (he stocks one of the widest and rarest selections in the city) that keeps fans returning.

GEM BY MOTO

Map 4; 1-30-9 Ebisu, Shibuya; ///coverage.fool.stumpy;
www.gembymoto.gorp.jp

As its name suggests, this is a local gem – so much so that reservations are mandatory to snag one of the few counter seats. Follow the after-work crowds and forgo the menu, leaving your evening and sake choices in the hands of the friendly manager, Marie Chiba.

» Don't leave without having the gorgonzola and mushroom risotto for dinner. It pairs wonderfully with sake.

ZOETROPE

Map 2; 3F, 7-10-14 Nishishinjuku, Shinjuku;
///lend.cities.molars; (03) 3363-0162

The only thing rivaling owner Atsushi Horigami's 300-bottle-strong whisky collection is his film library – luckily, he's not one to keep either to himself. An old-school vibe prevails at this laid-back spot, where spirit lovers sip rare Japanese whiskies while watching silent movies.

Coffee Shops

Relishing a rich cup of coffee is a daily ritual.
Whether it be from a traditional Japanese coffee
parlor (**kissaten**) *or a sleek café, caffeine in Tokyo*
has no limits – and neither does the love for it.

ARISE COFFEE ROASTERS

Map 3; 1-13-8 Hirano, Koto; ///workouts.smart.grades; www.arisecoffee.jp

A hum of chatter is always in the air here, where coffee aficionados catch up in what feels like an extension of their living room. Located in Tokyo's self-proclaimed "coffee town," Arise brews and roasts single-origin varieties in-house. You can purchase your favorite beans to take home, but given how homey the space is, you won't be in a rush to leave.

BALLON D'ESSAI LATTE & ART

Map 4; 2-30-11 Kitazawa, Setagaya;
///relax.offhand.richly; (03) 6804-7651

Thrift shoppers won't consider anywhere else for a refueling brew after scouring the streets of Shimokitazawa. Though they may hesitate to drink the coffee for fear of spoiling the beautiful latte art (the main draw here), they find the smell too intoxicating to resist.

CAFÉ DE L'AMBRE

Map 5; 8-10-15 Ginza, Chuo; ///intend.rings.pricing;
www.cafedelambre.com

Keeping Ginza locals caffeinated since 1948, this classic café is the definition of a Japanese *kissaten*, or retro-style coffee shop. Unlike modern places that pride themselves on fresh-roasted beans, this spot is known for its aged coffee beans, which add an extra depth in flavor. The menu consists only of coffee, but you don't need anything else.

» Don't leave without trying an iced coffee variety like the Blanc et Noir, served sweet in a champagne glass along with a touch of milk.

LITTLE DARLING COFFEE ROASTERS

Map 5; 1-12-32 Minamiaoyama, Minato;
///dandelions.flexed.stardom; www.littledarlingcoffeeroasters.com

Visit this coffee roaster often enough and you'll recognize the edgy regulars, spread out over the outdoor lawn (a rarity in central Tokyo) with their espressos. It's a laid-back hangout, housed in a former warehouse within the Share Green Minami Aoyama park complex.

Try it!
ENJOY A TASTING

To get more serious about your coffee, head to Koffee Mameya Kakeru *(www.koffee-mameya.com)* in Kiyosumi-Shirakawa and ask to sample a tasting course, where various roasts are served with small sweets.

LION

Map 1; 2-19-13 Dogenzaka, Shibuya;
///loaded.pockets.cones; (03) 3461-6858

Designed for audiophiles, this is far from a regular café. Sure, you can get a great coffee here, but it's all about the listening experience that enhances every sip: every booth faces the huge custom-made speakers, which blare out classical records from morning to night. There's a strict no-talking rule, which is strongly adhered to by the long-timers, students, and musicians who frequent this sacred spot.

MIA MIA

Map 6; 4-10-1 Nagasaki, Toshima;
///obvious.swinging.reporter; www.mia-mia.tokyo

Based on the notion that a coffee shop is more than just a spot to get a caffeine fix, Mia Mia is a true community hub built for locals to meet and exchange ideas – with a great cup of coffee, of course.

Shh!

Unbeknown to those who only drop by in the day and during the week, Mia Mia transforms from a café to a late-night bar on the weekends. It resembles something of an underground house party, when those in-the-know flick through the vinyl record collection and make a soundtrack request. Ask the staff for recommendations on the rotating selection of mostly Australian and Japanese wines and craft beers.

It's owned and run by a charismatic Japanese-Australian couple, who transformed a dilapidated boutique clothing store into a stylish retro-café, without the pretension. Expect young, inner-city professionals mingling with chatty retirees.

SATEI HATO

Map 1; 1-15-19 Shibuya, Shibuya; ///clashes.snipped.filed; (03) 3400-9088

Entering this classic Japanese *kissaten* is like taking a step back in time. It oozes old-school appeal, mostly thanks to the selection of vintage cups and saucers stacked behind the counter (you can pick your preferred set to have your coffee in). One of the last remaining vestiges of the past in a modernized Shibuya, this is where locals come to devote a few hours, savoring a coffee with a newspaper on a quiet table around the back.

» Don't leave without ordering a slice of the signature chiffon cake, which makes a perfect accompaniment to your cup of coffee.

HEART'S LIGHT COFFEE

Map 4; Hills Shibuya 1F, 13-13 Shinsencho, Shibuya; ///follow.knee.inclined; www.heartslightcoffee.stores.jp

Everything about this place is cool: stylish baristas, a copper coffee roaster, vinyl lining the walls. The only sounds you'll hear in this laid-back space are smooth tunes playing and aromatic coffee being dripped. If you like what you taste (and hear), purchase 200g of coffee beans and you'll get a complimentary record to take home.

Tearooms

Tea is a Japanese institution. The age-old tradition of drinking the good stuff is cherished in beautiful tearooms and modern cafés that keep this delicious practice alive.

GEN GEN AN BY EN TEA

Map 1; 4-8 Udagawacho, Shibuya; ///removing.robots.pushy; www.en-tea.com

Don't be deterred by the unassuming shopfront: this certainly is a proper tearoom, but one that doesn't have to be old-fashioned to attract crowds. Visit this casual spot in the late afternoon, when daytime green tea orders turn into evening tea cocktails. It's where Tokyo's cool kids make tea, well, cool.

KOSOAN

Map 4; 1-24-23 Jiyugaoka, Meguro; ///spins.moisture.theme; www.kosoan.co.jp

You could easily mistake this teahouse for a private residence, hidden as is it behind a yard full of greenery and blending into its residential street. In fact, even stepping inside feels like entering someone's house. You're directed to take your shoes off (a Japanese

Plan to visit Kosoan after taking a leisurely walk around trendy Jiyugaoka and visiting its many boutiques.

custom inside the home) and settle on tatami mats (another cultural tradition where you eat and drink sitting on the floor). It's truly divine.

SAKURAI

Map 1; Spiral Bldg 5F, 5-6-23 Minamiaoyama, Minato; ///frowns.guilty.uptake; www.sakurai-tea.jp

While many tearooms in Tokyo embrace the ancient art of the tea ceremony in a traditional setting, few have embraced it in a modern space like this spot. Founder Shinya Sakurai trained as a tea master for 14 years before opening this stylish shop in the hope of modernizing the culture and getting more people acquainted with the art – and he's been pretty successful in doing so. Prices are quite steep, but it's worth splashing out for the best-quality tea leaves and tasting courses.

IPPODO

Map 5; 3-1-1 Marunouchi, Chiyoda; ///hidden.mile.casually; www.ippodo-tea.co.jp

Ask any local where to find the best green tea in the city and they'll send you to this 300-year-old gem. Sure, you can grab a cup to go, but the best way to indulge in the tea's aromatic flavors is to slip past the counter to the Kaboku Tearoom, where a freshly whipped matcha is served with traditional *wagashi* sweets.

>> Don't leave without signing up for a free class in the tearoom to learn how to prepare a proper cup of green tea yourself.

HIGASHIYA
Map 5; Pola Ginza Bldg 2F, 1-7-7 Ginza, Chuo;
///line.misfits.raves; www.higashiya.com

You'll often see the well-dressed ladies of Ginza engaging in afternoon tea at this beautiful confectionery shop, which doubles as a tea salon overlooking the ritzy streets. Swinging by this sophisticated spot is an impressive move if you've got in-laws or parents in tow. And so is enriching your tea with the shop's handcrafted, bite-sized confections.

GROOVY NA OCHA
Map 4; 2-3-6 Higashiyama, Meguro;
///goodness.status.tornado; www.groovynaocha.jp

Forget pairing your tea with *wagashi* sweets for a moment. Nuts may be a somewhat unexpected match, but they're part and parcel with a cuppa at this one-of-a-kind tea shop. The chummy owner also helms a nut shop around the corner, and it wasn't long before he realized that nuts and tea have a commonality: a "deep taste created by Mother Earth." And so Groovy Na Ocha was born.

Try it!
TEA CEREMONY

Sign up for a traditional tea ceremony at Masuda-ya *(www.masuda-ya.co.jp)* in Shinjuku. It's the best way to learn the ins and outs of the ceremonial way of making, serving, and enjoying tea.

Dotting every table are bowls of raw walnuts that guests can crack into as they please, to balance the delicate aroma of tea. It won't be long before you're a convert and those bowls need a refill.

INARI TEA

Map 4; 1-5-2 Ebisu, Shibuya; ///supper.valid.scanning; www.inari-tea.jp

A café by day and a chic bar by night, Inari shows that tea is not limited to daytime drinking. Strike up a chat with the friendly owner and it'll be early evening before you know it – not staying for a tea-infused cocktail would, quite frankly, be rude.

» Don't leave without pairing your drink with a roasted green tea tiramisu. (Maybe avoid having a green tea with it, for fear of overload.)

TOKYO SARYO

Map 4; 1-34-15 Kamiuma, Setagaya; ///bangle.basis.callers; www.tokyosaryo.jp

It's no secret that coffee is becoming more popular with Tokyo's young crowds than traditional teas, but this contemporary parlor is on a mission to change that. The tea equivalent of third-wave coffee shops (which prioritize the quality of taste), Tokyo Saryo has evolved the art of making tea to one that's actually akin to pour-over coffee. It's all about what they call "hand drip tea": carefully pouring hot water over tea leaves using coffee-style hand drippers. Yes, it's pretty unusual, but it results in the cleanest brew. Start with the tea-tasting experience, where you'll compare the flavor profiles of different single-origin varieties.

An afternoon
sampling sake

Sake is more than just a drink – it's ceremonious (heck, there's even a World Sake Day in October). During the Heian period (794–1185), Japan's national alcoholic beverage – made from rice, water, and yeast – was reserved for celebrations, and though it's widely available today, drinking it is still ritualistic. It's traditionally served warm in small ceramic cups, accompanied by Japanese food, and often poured with a bit of education from passionate sommeliers. You can't sip the stuff without swotting up on how to do it properly.

AKASAKA

ROPPONGI

AZABU-JUBAN

MINAMI-AZABU

1. JSS Information Center
1-6-15 Nishishinbashi, Minato; www.japan sake.or.jp
///rooftop.panthers.puts

2. Shiba Toshogu
4-8-10 Shibakoen, Minato; www.shibatoshogu.com
///coolest.beeline.bank

3. Tokyo Port Brewery
4-7-10 Shiba, Minato
///advice.footsteps.fields

4. SAKE Scene
1F, 2-11-20 Shibadaimon, Minato; www.sake scene.com
///masking.cases.fraction

5. Kuri
Sakurai Bldg 2F, 3-19-4 Shinbashi, Minato;
(03) 3573-8033
///pets.district.wheels

Sake Hall Hibiya Bar
///moving.scanner.battling

**Get acquainted at the
JSS INFORMATION CENTER**

Take a hands-on crash course
on everything there is to know
about sake, like the ideal
temperature to drink it at.

1

Sake Hall Hibiya Bar
*is the world's first bar
and shop specializing in
sake-based cocktails.
The bartenders use sake
from all over Japan.*

GINZA

5 **Have a drink at
KURI**

Put your knowledge to
good use and peruse
100 different varieties
at this bar to find your
perfect match.

NISHI-
SHINBASHI

SHINBASHI

ATAGO

HIGASHI-
SHINBASHI

ABUDAI

HIBIYA · DORI

DAIICHI · KEIHIN

*Hama Rikyu
Garden*

SHIBA-
KOEN

SHIBA-
DAIMON

HAMAMATSUCHO

**Pay homage at
SHIBA TOSHOGU**

Drinking sake is thought to
bring people closer to the
gods. Buy some sake from
a nearby store and leave it
as an offering at this shrine
in a show of respect.

2

HIBIYA · DORI

SHIBA

DAIICHI · KEIHIN

4 **Become an expert at
SAKE SCENE**

Thirsty to learn more? Chat to owner
Yukari Yanaba about which dishes
pair well with sake while she warms
up a cup of the good stuff for you.

**Snoop around
TOKYO PORT BREWERY**

Tour Tokyo's only inner-city sake
brewery, witness how the drink is
made, and enjoy a sampling
session when you're finished.

3

0 meters		500
0 yards		500

SHOP

Tokyo's stores are a celebration of its locals. Anime havens, specialty gourmet stores, and jam-packed vintage shops reflect a city of niche interests and immense collectors.

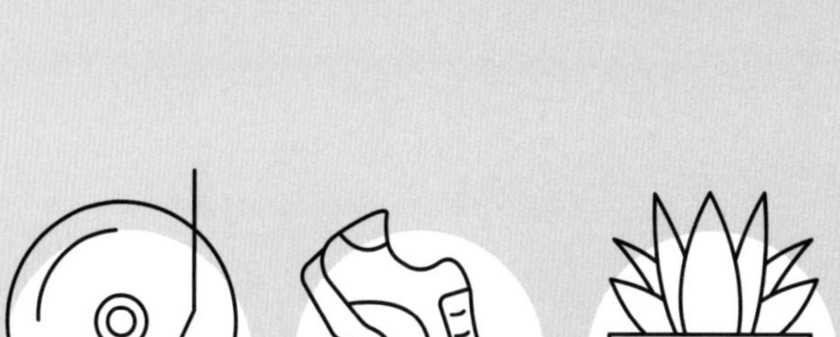

Record Stores

Dusty warehouses housing even dustier vinyl or minimal inner-city stores selling the coolest new releases: it doesn't matter how it's showcased, if it's music in collectible form, Tokyoites go wild for it.

FLASH DISC RANCH

Map 4; 2F, 2-12-16 Kitazawa, Setagaya; ///siblings.jiffy.struggle; (03) 3414-0421

The philosophy here is simple: good music at a good price. There's nothing showy about this messy warehouse-esque space, packed to the rafters with records. Affable owner Masao Tsubaki (whose cool energy filters out into the space) speaks a bit of English, if you need advice on which boxes to sift through. In short, it's where to stock up on mint-condition favorites and dusty classics without going broke.

RECORD SHOP BASE

Map 6; 4-23-5 Koenjiminami, Suginami; ///starting.drifter.intent; www.recordshopbase.com

Koenji used to be the epicenter of Tokyo's punk scene, and Record Shop Base is still keeping the flame of anarchy alive (with the addition of warm customer service). Giving off the feel of an underground club with posters filling every inch of wall and ceiling space, this is the kind of place where you'll find grungy musicians with a guitar strapped to their back digging out heavy metal records and CDs.

LIGHTHOUSE RECORDS

Map 1; Seijitsu Bldg 4F, 2-9-2 Dogenzaka, Shibuya;
///notched.rods.desire; www.lighthouserecords.jp

If your favourite album is one that your best mate recommended, this is the vinyl store for you. Owner Yasuharu has been building a record collection since he was 18 years old, and his love for the art of collecting, and music itself, speaks volumes. Here, every record on display – be it house, techno, disco, funk, soul – has a handwritten note attached to it, offering up Yasuharu's personal description and review. Expect to leave cradling a new favourite (sorry, best mate).

» Don't leave without testing out a handful of records at one of the listening stations to see if your musical merits align with Yasuharu's.

Shh!

A tiny hole-in-the-wall record shop in Koenji, EAD *(www. eadrecord.com)* is where vinyl lovers in-the-know come for quality secondhand records that span dance and house, afrobeat, and jazz funk.

Owner Yoso-san is incredibly knowledgeable about music, and one of the best things about coming here is to hear his recommendations on both vinyls to buy and underground music spots to visit nearby.

DISK UNION SHINJUKU
Map 2; Yamada Bldg, 3-31-4 Shinjuku, Shinjuku; ///obvious.shields.zoom;
www.diskunion.net

In a city of over 700 record stores, you'd think to avoid the chains and head straight for the niche gems. However, there's a lot to be said for this unofficial flagship branch of Japan's main indie record store. It's an absolute monolith, where vinyl hunters of all persuasions make for one of the eight genre-segregated floors of their choice, on the hunt for the best-priced new rock releases or secondhand Latin records. A must-visit for all self-respecting music fans.

WALTZ
Map 4; 4-15-5 Nakameguro, Meguro;
///puddles.cheeses.safely; www.waltz-store.co.jp

Stocking vintage merch, vinyl records, cassettes (yep, they're alive and well here), and boomboxes, Waltz is as much a store as an archive of musical history. Retro-hip tastemakers and devoted collectors lose themselves in the sleek space, where chairs are set up beside listening stations and a sense of 1980s nostalgia prevails.

CITY COUNTRY CITY
Map 4; Hosozawa Bldg 4F, 2-12-13 Kitazawa, Setagaya;
///happier.revives.soap; www.city-country-city.com

Hidden inside an office building, this rustic store is a hangout for an in-crowd of creatives. A DJ spins tracks in the corner (they take record requests) and an on-site bar keeps you drinking until 1am (it serves

Make a night of it and have dinner at the on-site café. The pasta is the most raved-about dish.

non-alcoholic bevs, too), so shopping here feels like rummaging through your friend's record collection at a house party. It's effortlessly cool.

BIG LOVE RECORDS

Map 2; 2-31-3 Jingumae, Shibuya; ///animated.hills.loses;
www.bigloverecords.jp

A renowned destination for those on a Japan-wide record store pilgrimage, this cool spot has developed a cult-like following with indie bands and travelers. Despite global accolades, it's dedicated to maintaining an independent image and keeping the underground music scene alive. Crate-digging fanatics come to scout through the vinyl releases, cassettes, CDs, and zines for a limited-run find.

» Don't leave without relaxing with a Japanese Shiga Kogen craft beer in the on-site bar after perusing the crates.

MANHATTAN RECORDS

Map 1; 10-1 Udagawacho, Shibuya;
///cotton.pictured.stunning; www.manhattanrecords.jp

Sitting in a graffiti-covered corner of backstreet Shibuya, this store has been a centerpiece of the hip-hop community for over three decades. Unsure what to buy? The shop's passionate staff, many of whom are local DJs, spin their current favorites on the in-house decks during their shifts – have a listen while you browse the rap, RnB, and funk lining the shelves, then purchase the record that gives you the most feels.

Edible Gifts

Gourmet gift-giving is an integral part of Japanese culture, where tokens of appreciation are given when visiting a friend's house or attending a congratulatory event. Luckily, shops are dedicated to this pastime.

AKOMEYA

Map 3; 67 Yaraicho, Shinjuku; ///directs.cuff.mason; www.akomeya.jp
If there's one staple ingredient you'll find in every Japanese household or restaurant storecupboard, it's rice. This simple carb has never been so on trend (or exciting) thanks to Akomeya, where grains are sold in bulk and wrapped in tasteful packaging. You'll come to stock up on key ingredients and leave with a stylish rice cooker to give to your parents or in-laws.

Try it!
CRAFT A CARD

You'll need a card for your gifts, so why not book onto a traditional *shodo* (calligraphy) workshop at Tokyo Calligraphy Class (*www. tokyocalligraphyclass.com*)? You'll learn how to hold the brush and draw basic characters.

KAYANOYA

Map 3; Coredo Muromachi 3, 1-5-5 Nihonbashimuromachi, Chuo;
///widest.gums.broccoli; www.kayanoya.com

Beloved by top (and budding) chefs, the flagship store of this soy sauce brewery carries an astonishing array of condiments – all of which you can sample before purchasing. Can't decide? Enlist a soy specialist and they'll likely direct you to a seasoning you never knew existed.

NUMBER SUGAR

Map 1; 5-11-11 Jingumae, Shibuya; ///arrived.alleges.hurls;
www.numbersugar.jp

Receiving a box of decadent caramels from this shop always goes down well. Caramels aren't a common Japanese sweet, but you'll find them in playful flavors like matcha and miso here, all packaged in stylish boxes that giftees won't ever want to part with.

» Don't leave without ordering a caramel smoothie, made using all natural ingredients and without a hint of sickliness to the taste.

DAIMARU TOKYO

Map 5; 1-9-1 Marunouchi, Chiyoda; ///painted.list.insect;
www.daimaru.co.jp/tokyo

Attached to Tokyo Station, this department store is a savior when you're after a thoughtful gift before you hop on a train to see an old friend. Trawl through two floors of gourmet treats, pick up a box of chocolates, and make a pitstop at "bento street" to grab a bento box for your journey (well, you need to treat yourself, too).

MATTERHORN

Map 4; 3-5-1 Takaban, Meguro; ///minds.awake.outsiders;
www.matterhorn-tokyo.com

This decades-old cake shop holds a special place in the hearts of many Tokyoites, who often came by with their grandparents as a kid for a birthday treat. It remains the go-to spot for special occasion gifts, where decadent cakes make for perfect engagement party fodder and buttery cookies in cute tins are worthy of any dinner party.

MITSUKOSHI NIHOMBASHI

Map 3; 1-4-1 Nihonbashimuromachi, Chuo;
///breath.prefix.synthetic; www.mitsukoshi.mistore.jp

You're never far from a *depachika* in Tokyo – food halls located in the basements of the city's many department stores. This one stands out above the rest, however, when locals are seeking seriously high-end gourmet gifts made to impress. The basement brims with a

Shh!

While locals fill out the famed Mitsukoshi Nihombashi department store, a small crowd of those in-the-know head across to Nihonbashi Imoya Kinjiro *(www.imokin. co.jp)*, an oft-overlooked shop specializing in fresh-fried candied sweet-potato snacks. Watch the fascinating cooking process from the store windows and then head inside to nab a free sample before making your purchase.

number of stylish food stalls where you can pick up the likes of mochi rice cakes, traditional sweets, and alcohol from well-known brands, all wrapped up in stunning packaging.

KITKAT CHOCOLATORY

Map 1; Miyashita Park South 2F, 6-20-10 Jingumae, Shibuya; ///rigid.betrayed.cooking; www.nestle.jp

There's something smug about shopping for KitKats here, knowing you'll leave with premium flavors like matcha and yuzu sake that you can't get anywhere else. Interestingly, KitKats act like amulets for students taking exams (the brand's name sounds a lot like *kitto katsu*, which means good luck), so purchase a few wacky flavors for the teens in your life and save the slightly alcoholic varieties for yourself.

» Don't leave without visiting the café, where you can tuck into beautiful desserts made with – you guessed it – KitKats.

TORAYA

Map 5; 4-9-22 Akasaka, Minato; ///brittle.cascade.unscrew; www.global.toraya-group.co.jp

It's pretty much expected to bring a beautifully presented box of *wagashi* sweets home from Japan. And there's nowhere better to shop for these traditional teatime sweets than at the flagship shop of the traditional confectionery purveyor, Toraya. The sweets, which are little pieces of artwork, change according to the season, so your family and friends back home can look forward to cherry blossom-flavored (and shaped) sweets in the spring or robust chestnut items during the fall.

Otaku Shops

Japan is the undisputed home of anime and manga. Otaku (geek) shops are not only merchandise outlets for these genres: they're playgrounds for passionate fans who live and breathe this world.

MANDARAKE

Map 6; Lions Mansion Ikebukuro B1F, 3-15-2 Higashiikebukuro, Toshima; ///cabin.benched.gold; www.mandarake.co.jp

The nicknamed *Otome* (maiden) Road in Ikebukuro is known as a girl geek's paradise, given that many of its stores focus on the series with largely female fanbases. It's fitting, then, that this is where you'll find Mandarake and its impressive female-oriented manga library. Expect fans pouring over one of the largest collections of *doujinshi* (anime by amateurs) and the highly popular *yaoi* or "Boys Love" genre.

POKÉMON CENTER

Map 1; Shibuya Parco 6F, 15-1 Udagawacho, Shibuya; ///empires.fills.tunnel; www.pokemon.co.jp

If seeing Tokyoites playing Pokémon Go on street corners is anything to go by, it's safe to say they're obsessed with the franchise. And to get their Poké-fix, fans of all ages come to this store to get lost in the sea

Pokémon-obsessed fans should also visit the Pokémon Café in Nihonbashi for fun themed dishes.

of playing cards, figurines, stationery, sweets – the list goes on. It's stocked full of exclusive Japan merchandise, so there's no excuse to not catch 'em all.

NAKANO BROADWAY

Map 2; 5-52-15 Nakano, Nakano; ///monkeys.bumpy.pints; www.nakano-broadway.com

There's always a frenetic energy at this empire of a shopping mall, Tokyo's hub for hardcore anime lovers. Packed floor-to-ceiling with as much memorabilia as possible, each store (there's about 300) is a goldmine for those seeking rare finds. Looking for that elusive Pokémon card? There's a shop for that. Age-old Star Wars toys? You'll find those in spades too.

» **Don't leave without** grabbing a colorful eight-layered rainbow ice cream at Daily Chiko, located in the basement food court.

VILLAGE VANGUARD

Map 1; B1F-2F, 23–3 Udagawacho, Shibuya; ///wires.walnuts.elects; www.village-v.co.jp

This huge general goods store is a mega-outlet of Japanese geek culture. One minute you're browsing dinosaur backpacks; the next, novelty sweets; before you know it, an hour has passed and you haven't even made it to the Mario Kart merch section you came in for. With office workers and school kids lining up at the cash register, the store's clientele is as varied as its wares.

NINTENDO STORE

Map 1; Shibuya Parco 6F, 15-1 Udagawacho, Shibuya;
///deciding.hint.hiding; www.nintendo.co.jp

It's safe to say Nintendo's fanbase outsizes this massive store, Japan's first and only shop for the video game company. In fact, excitable shoppers stand in line for hours, praying to get their hands on exclusive characters and gaming merchandise. Well, you won't find Animal Crossing kitchen gear and Zelda business attire anywhere else.

DORAEMON FUTURE DEPARTMENT STORE

Map 5; DiverCity Tokyo Plaza 2F, 1-1-10 Aomi, Koto, Odaiba;
///goad.doormat.crisps; www.mirai.dora-world.com

Only in Tokyo would you find a store dedicated to a single anime character. Enter Doraemon, the blue cat-robot who has captured the hearts of many since the 1970s. Show your love by personalizing a Doraemon bag or towel, then check out the game center.

THE GUNDAM BASE TOKYO

Map 5; DiverCity Tokyo Plaza 7F, 1-1-10 Aomi, Koto;
///active.sneezed.both; www.gundam-base.net

The center of the Gundam sci-fi anime franchise is more than your average shop. It's practically a museum, where fans of all ages come to ogle 1,500 giant battle bot models before choosing which to purchase from an even steeper 2,000.

>> Don't leave without taking a tour of the factory zone, where machinery and molds let you see how the bots are made.

Liked by the locals

"The Nintendo Store is the best because they have huge screens where you can test out new video games. Everyone in the store can see you, but it's so fun."

LINDSAY ARAKAWA, CREATIVE AND SOCIAL MEDIA
STRATEGIST AND NINTENDO FAN

Home Touches

Beautifully curated homeware stores are a visible expression of Japan's craftsmanship. Locals love filling their homes with unique pieces (and getting interior inspo from these cool shops, too).

KIYA SHOP

Map 5; Tokyo Midtown Galleria 3F, 9-7-4 Akasaka, Minato;
///advances.snacks.blazers; www.kiya-hamono.co.jp

It feels like you're shopping for fine jewelry rather than kitchen utensils at this sleek, minimal store. Japanese knives are displayed so neatly on the walls that you'll hesitate to remove them, let alone use them. But you need something to slice your sushi perfectly, right?

» Don't leave without buying a traditional wooden bento box, the beloved piece of kitchenwear that defines Japan.

CINQ

Map 6; 2-28-3 Kichijojihoncho, Musashino;
///postage.romance.threaten; www.cinq-design.com

Typifying the Japanese concept of *zakka*, this miscellaneous goods store aims to celebrate the ordinary. Purchasing cleaning supplies and kitchenwear may feel mundane, but Cinq's items – sourced from Europe and Japan – are so lovely, you can't help but feel excited shopping for them. Teapots and woven baskets are also displayed in such a beautiful manner that rushing home to imitate the shop's aesthetics is a given. And that's what *zakka* is all about – the journey of searching for practical objects and making them beautiful in your own home, in turn bringing you joy.

BLUE & WHITE

Map 5; 2F, 2-9-2 Azabujuban, Minato; ///mobile.mimics.hung;
www.blueandwhitejapan.com

You know you've arrived at Blue & White when these are the only two colors in your direct vision. The bright and homely space is run by an American expat, Amy Katoh, who has made it her mission to seduce shoppers (many of whom are fellow expats) with beautiful handicrafts from all around Japan. The color scheme is no accident – indigo-dyed products reflect Japan's ancient method of working with fabric. So, whether you buy a custom-designed hand towel or a ceramic, it all oozes national pride.

Try it!
STITCH AND SEW

Get in touch with your artistic side and sign up for a *sashiko* stitching workshop at Blue & White. This traditional sewing technique can be used to accent the likes of clothing and tablecloths.

YUMIKO IIHOSHI PORCELAIN

Map 4; SPT Bldg 1-A, 6-6 Daikanyamacho, Shibuya;
///heap.upper.elevate; www.y-iihoshi-p.com

Minimalists flock to this calming, sleek space to pick up the latest item crafted by Yumiki Iihoshi. A well-loved pottery and ceramic artist, Iihoshi is loved for her simple yet modern porcelain designs – dinner plates, mugs, serving platters, and teapots in beautiful, muted colors that incorporate well into any and every home. You won't be able to resist hosting dinner parties to show them all off.

SIPPO

Map 6; 1-18-25 Kichijoji Kitamachi, Musashino;
///tigers.candles.croak; www.sippo-4.com

Though hidden down a residential street, Sippo is easy enough to find: just look for the locals checking out the antique tablewear outside. But don't get too distracted yourself out there, as a whole other world of knick-knacks – from crockery to socks – awaits inside. If you find yourself gazing longingly at the table holding all the stock, you'll be glad to know even that's for sale.

KINTO

Map 4; 1-19-12 Aobadai, Meguro; ///savers.fuels.tens;
www.kinto.co.jp

You'd be hard-pressed to find a local who doesn't carry one of Kinto's handy, reusable tumblers in hand as they go about their day in the city. These beloved tumblers – which come in various sizes and

Join a fun flower-arranging class at Kinto, then buy a vase in-store to display your new blooms in.

colors – don't just hold cold drinks, but also have fab heat retention to keep your coffee warm. Speaking of coffee, why not buy a stylish carafe set to make it in, too?

COTOGOTO

Map 6; 2F, 4-27-17 Koenjiminami, Suginami; ///heads.trooper.grit; www.cotogoto.jp

Japan loves a bit of wooden tableware, and that's where this homeware store really shines. Among the shelves of bamboo baskets and earthenware pots are delicately handcrafted bowls and mugs, made using the finest wood. They're timeless, rustic staples needed to recreate the traditional Japanese dining experience at home.

D&DEPARTMENT

Map 6; 8-3-2 Okusawa, Setagaya; ///ordering.device.approach; www.d-department.com

Nearly everything about this shop is sustainable, from the upcycled home goods to the recycled shopping bags donated by other shoppers. More specifically, though, the store specializes in offering items from all 47 prefectures of Japan – simply look at the label to see where each product originates and what year it was created. It's a haven for eco-conscious folk who come to invest in lust-worthy, mid-century furniture and practical homewares.

» Don't leave without joining the other shoppers with a cup of tea and a cake at the calming on-site café.

Street Style

*In a city where tradition holds strong, street fashion
has nonetheless allowed Tokyo's youth a form of
self-expression for decades. It's all about making a
fashion statement through cool, casual clothing.*

HAVE A GOOD TIME

**Map 4; 1-4-18 Nakameguro, Meguro; ///mildest.qualified.various;
www.have-a-goodtime.com**

Equal parts cheeky, friendly, and cool, this is the back alley store all
fashion-conscious skaters dream of owning one day. It's run by a
tight-knit Tokyo crew, who also have a clothing label under the name
("Have a Good Time" is plastered all over the t-shirts and hoodies).
As well as branded items, skater kids can find collaboration pieces
with the likes of streetwear empires Vans, Stussy, and BEAMS.

NEW YORK JOE EXCHANGE

**Map 4; 3-26-4 Kitazawa, Setagaya; ///ports.dampen.parent;
www.newyorkjoeexchange.com**

Think locals only trade Pokémon cards? Think again. Exchanging
unwanted clothes for in-store credit is the name of the game here —
given the staff think your used apparel is cool enough, mind. That's

because New York Joe Exchange is hipster at its core: it's set inside an old Japanese bathhouse, attracting a young crowd for the industrial-chic decor as much as the grungy clothing. Recycling has never been so on trend.

RAGTAG

Map 1; 6-14-2 Jingumae, Shibuya; ///engages.wings.dolphins; www.ragtag.jp

It's easy to mistake this classy shop for a high-end store, filled with designer garms. The big difference is that the labels come without the outrageous price tags (and the sometimes dusty smell of secondhand clothing). While the fashion-conscious sift the racks of hot international labels on the first floor, style mavens check out the accessories from coveted Japanese designers on the second.

» Don't leave without heading up to the third floor, dedicated to high-end designer handbags from labels like Gucci and Chanel.

SAMVA

Map 4; 2-5 Daikanyamacho, Shibuya; ///puff.sports.samples; www.samva.hiphop

This boutique is home to the beloved Japanese label Yeah Right!!, which is leading the way in the city's sustainable fashion movement. It's attracted a cult-like following for upcycled pieces, made by reworking preloved clothing and homewares in innovative ways. Everything from used scarves to rugs becomes cushions and T-shirts, so you're allowed to feel smug as you redecorate your home and wardrobe sustainably.

HAYATOCHIRI

Map 6; 3-4-11 Kitakoenji, Suginami; ///frames.saucepan.diner;
www.hayatochiri.thebase.in

You know you're in for something special when the owner of a store is quoted for wanting to create "the most interesting place in the world!" He's pretty close to achieving it, too. This iconic fashion store sits somewhere between cartoonish hideout, its walls lined with manga book tear-outs, and designer atelier on acid, where LED lights are handsewn into preloved jackets. It's an eccentric delight, where you can always find a bold DIY statement piece.

ATMOS

Map 5; 3-3-14 Ginza, Chuo; ///alien.mission.wooden;
www.atmos-tokyo.com

A shrine to the humble sneaker, the famed Atmos store takes its merch very seriously. You won't find any old shoe on the shelves here. The stock is as carefully curated as the walls, where colorful kicks are artfully displayed in a floor-to-ceiling gallery. With shoes

Try it!
DESIGNER FOR THE DAY

Stand out from the crowd and customize a pair of made-in-Japan shoes at Tokyo's Converse White Atelier (www.whiteatelier-by-converse.jp). You'll be able to add text and patterns, and choose your own laces.

ranging from the hottest brands on the market to the most stylish (and practical) runners for working out, Atmos is where obsessive sneakerheads go when they're after the latest designs.

NEIGHBORHOOD

Map 1; 4-32-7 Jingumae, Shibuya; ///prompting.resold.tablets; www.neighborhood.jp

It's fitting that this pioneering shop is located in Harajuku, given that the area is the home of Tokyo's streetwear aesthetic. Neighborhood is easily one of Japan's most influential labels – you only need to stroll through Harajuku to see its shirts and hoodies donning most creatives. Expect a cool clientele shopping for clothes that blend the likes of London's teddy-boy culture and New York's hip-hop scene.

KINJI

Map 1; Tokyo YM Square Harajuku B1F, 4-31-10 Jingumae, Shibuya; ///curl.sagging.normal; www.kinji.jp

When the cool kids of Harajuku want to get rid of their cast-offs, they give it all to Kinji. And when they want to pick up someone else's, they head right back. There's an inclusivity to this massive store, where goths, rockabilies, and everyone in between is guaranteed to find something in their size and to their taste. Aside from the latest trends, Kinji also stocks used designer and non-designer wares, as well as costume jewelry and even a small selection of pre-worn kimono.

» Don't leave without sifting through Kinji's rack of reasonably priced Japanese souvenir jackets, also known as a *sukajan*.

SENDAGI

NISHI-NIPPORI

Swot up at
YANESEN TOURIST INFORMATION & CULTURE CENTER

There's an art to wearing a kimono. Learn about the layers, multiple ties, and ideal length required with the help of specialists here.

Stock up at
MIDORIYA

Bamboo has long been used to make products in Japan, and everything at this home store is made of the strong, flexible wood. Purchase some chopsticks – they're essential.

GOTEN - ZAKA

YANAKA - GINZA

① **②** **③**

Performances of amezaiku – a candy-craft artistry dating back to the 700s – take place daily at Amezaiku Yoshihara.

Have a browse at
YANAKA MATSUNOYA

You can't miss this store, its handwoven baskets spilling out onto the street. Pore over the goods inside, too: utensils, homeware, and more.

YOMISE - DORI

ROKU - AMIDA - MICHI

SANSAKISAKA - DORI

④

⑤

Peruse the gallery-like
SONOMITSU

There's no going back to regular shoes once you've tried a handcrafted pair at this store. Avoid waiting six months for a bespoke pair and get a ready-to-wear style.

YANAKA

Get crafty at
NEKOEMON CAFÉ

Originating in Japan, the *maneki neko* (beckoning cat) is thought to bring good luck. Take charge of your fortune and make one at this workshop.

SENDAGI

0 meters	200
0 yards	200

NEZU

An afternoon shopping in
old-school Yanesen

Craftsmanship defines Japan and Tokyo's artisans, hailed "Living National Treasures," have been perfecting and selling their crafts over multiple generations in Yanesen, a fusion of three areas – Yanaka, Nezu, and Sendagi – that retains the charm of the Edo period (1603–1868). A relaxed pace defines shopping here, where time-honored snack stores and traditional homeware shops take up space in rustic buildings.

NISHI-NIPPORI

YANAKA

Yanaka Cemetery

A cluster of well-preserved Edo-style buildings, built nearly 80 years ago, lie in **Ueno Sakuragi Atari**. *They now house shops.*

UENO-KURAGI

TOTOI - DORI

1. Yanesen Tourist Information & Culture Center
3-13-7 Yanaka, Taito;
www.ti-yanesen.jp/
experience/kimono
///humidity.earful.linen

2. Midoriya
3-13-3 Nishinippori,
Arakawa; (03) 3828 7522
///coast.quit.stapled

3. Yanaka Matsunoya
3-14-14 Nishinippori,
Arakawa; www.yanaka
matsunoya.jp
///logs.debater.slam

4. Sonomitsu
2-18-6 Yanaka, Taito;
www.sonomitsu.com
///prompting.loaf.costumes

5. Nekoemon Café
5-4-2 Yanaka, Taito;
(03) 3821-0090
///pocket.swimmer.payer

Amezaiku Yoshihara
///sulked.awaited.moment

Ueno Sakuragi Atari
///times.basic.gearbox

ARTS & CULTURE

Tokyo's cultural scene is a microcosm of the city at large. Traditions are nurtured, yet boundaries are pushed across the likes of art, technology, and sport.

Contemporary Art

The world may clamor over Japan's more traditional art forms (think ukiyo-e prints and screen paintings), but locals equally love to engage with the vibrant modern art scene and the innovators shaping it.

NANZUKA

Map 2; 3-31-10 Jingumae, Shibuya; ///butter.asking.grower; www.nug.jp

Once the new kid on the block, Nanzuka has become a powerhouse in the contemporary art scene (it's still got a youthful, rebellious spirit though). Showcasing enigmatic and kaleidoscopic works by unknown artists, the space has become a magnet for art students. It's all about absorbing the city's electrifying and unconventional energy.

MORI ART MUSEUM

Map 5; Mori Tower 53F, 6-10-1 Roppongi, Minato; ///coffee.rocker.amends; www.mori.art.museum.com

While school groups and tour guides take over Mori in the day, this sky-high museum belongs to young creatives come evening. Sure, the thought-provoking exhibitions – ranging from installations to multimedia displays – are best explored without the crowds, but the

The rooftop Sky Deck hosts cool star-gazing parties. Check online before you visit to try to catch one.

real nightly draw is the Sky Deck. When you finish trawling the galleries, follow the locals to this rooftop, reflect with a cocktail, and marvel at the glittering dark sky.

SCAI THE BATHHOUSE

Map 3; 6-1-23 Yanaka, Taito; ///bedroom.mammoth.prance;
www.scaithebathhouse.com

You may not expect to find contemporary art inside a 200-year-old bathhouse, but as locals will tell you, Tokyo's art scene is far from ordinary. Located in an area that epitomizes Old Tokyo, SCAI dares to promote the new, showcasing up-and-coming artists and modern icons like Tatsuo Miyajima. It's a sacred affair, where paintings line neutral walls and natural light filters perfectly on cool installations.

TOKYO METROPOLITAN ART MUSEUM

Map 3; 8-36 Uenokoen, Taito; ///robot.hours.checked; www.tobikan.jp

It says a lot about this spot that, almost a century after it opened, locals still flock to exhibition openings. The nation's first public art museum labels itself as a "doorway to art," encouraging all walks of life to interact with all types of artwork. Strongly supporting this mission is the annual Ueno Artist Project; held from November to January, it's where local contemporary artists come together to exhibit their work, and the city's people lap it all up.

» Don't leave without indulging in some *yoshoku* (Western-style Japanese food) from the museum's Restaurant Muse.

COMPLEX 665

Map 5; 6-5-24 Roppongi, Minato; ///driver.chin.country; www.tohokuandtokyo.org/spot_177

Contemporary art lovers are spoiled for choice with the three galleries inside this building. Avant-garde advocate? Head to ShugoArts, where freedom of self-expression reigns. Seeking some new blood on the modern art scene? Tomio Koyama Gallery showcases eclectic, emerging Japanese artists. Camera-clad photography fan? Let the photos speak for themselves at Taka Ishii Gallery.

THE NATIONAL ART CENTER, TOKYO

Map 5; 7-22-2 Roppongi, Minato; ///solve.helpers.voltage; www.nact.jp

If the rippling glass facade is anything to go by, the huge National Art Center knows how to make an impact. It doesn't draw crowds through a permanent collection (unusually, there isn't one), but rather rotating exhibitions and thought-provoking artist talks. An

Shh!

Located near the National Art Center is s+arts *(www.splusarts. com)*, a small modern art gallery that is only really well known to industry insiders and a pool of curators and buyers. Aside from showcasing a number of talented Japanese artists, the gallery takes part in global art fairs and hosts a number of exhibitions. It's not a pretentious place, though – those who aren't making waves in the art world won't feel out of place.

inspiration hub, this is where resourceful students file into the art library and families enjoy the diverse shows that cover everything from anime to architecture. It's easy to lose an entire day among the twelve galleries inside, so when you come up for air, find a spot to relax and muse on the lawns.

21_21 DESIGN SIGHT

Map 5; 9-7-6 Akasaka, Minato; ///somebody.haven.prepared; www.2121designsight.jp

Initiated by fashion guru Issey Miyake, graphic designer Taku Satoh, and product designer Naoto Fukazawa, this museum was born out of the need for a space that promoted Japanese design. And devotees can't get enough of it, passing through for conceptual exhibitions, inspiring performances, and crafty workshops.

YAYOI KUSAMA MUSEUM

Map 2; 107 Bentencho, Shinjuku; ///duty.torch.steers; www.yayoikusamamuseum.jp

No trip to Tokyo would be complete without seeing some art by the legendary Yayoi Kusama – queen of pumpkins and polka dots – at the first museum dedicated to Japan's favorite avant-garde artist. During the week, intellectuals and curious curators mingle between events and lectures; as soon as the weekend hits, art and fashion students pack in for some design inspiration.

» Don't leave without visiting the wonderful washrooms – a work of art themselves, covered in Kusama's iconic polka dots.

Interactive Spaces

Robots more up your street than ancient ruins? Good news: Tokyo's cultural spaces aren't your usual institutions. At these playhouses of technology, forward-thinking reigns and locals step into the future.

KONICA MINOLTA PLANETARIA TOKYO

Map 5; Yurakucho Mullion 9-10F, 2-5-1 Yurakucho, Chiyoda; ///pity.steams.submits; www.planetarium.konicaminolta.jp

Tokyo is full of VR attractions that propel you into unknown worlds, but sometimes, it's the world we already live in that creates the most eye-widening moments. Cue this two-domed planetarium, which gets you closer to outer space through the use of the very latest technology (well, this is Tokyo). Dome 2 is all about stargazing, with projections of

---

Try it!
ENTER A SMALL WORLD

Want to leave a piece of you in Tokyo? Visit Small Worlds Tokyo *(www.smallworlds.jp)* and use the 3D scanner to make a 1:80 scale model of yourself. It'll live in the world of miniature attractions for a year.

a realistic starry sky gracing the ceiling, and cosy sofas to watch on from. Dome 1, however, does things a little differently – whether it's combining live music with a talk about space, or hosting seasonal events like 360-degree cherry blossom viewing.

» **Don't leave without** visiting the café for an extraordinary treat, from donuts glazed to look like a starry sky to drinks that glow.

MIRAIKAN

Map 5; 2-3-6 Aomi, Koto; ///urban.inquest.graphics;
www.miraikan.jst.go.jp

Think of Japan and you're probably picturing futuristic inventions. At the National Museum of Emerging Science and Innovation (or Miraikan, as locals know it), high-tech creations are exactly what you get. Curious science students and technology fanatics regularly frequent this game-esque space to be amazed, educated, and even a little freaked out. The exhibit they always head to first? The hypnotizing Robots in Your Life, where the line between human and robot is questioned. Welcome to the future: you're living in it.

TOKYO TRICK ART MUSEUM

Map 5; DECKS Tokyo Beach 4F, 1-6-1, Daiba, Minato;
///collect.once.totals; www.trickart.info

At this gallery of optical illusions, 2D painting scenes are created to look 3D – and you're invited to become part of them by posing in front. Whether trapped under a glass by a vampire or regaining agency by fighting ninjas, your visual senses are set to be bewildered.

TEPIA

Map 2; 2-8-44 Kitaaoyama, Minato; ///arrival.risen.animal; www.tepia.jp

In a city where out-of-towners love to lap up the ideas of the future, there are some forward-thinking museums that locals like to keep to themselves. This under-the-radar museum is one of them, and despite its lack of renown (rarely listed in guidebooks and meekly promoted in English), it's regarded by its regular visitors as one of the best science attractions in the city. Focusing on social issues like future living and an aging society, it's a space where the curious come to learn about the world developing before them. Get a full-body scan and a reading of your stress levels (they should be low, given the lack of crowds here), learn how automated mobility pushers could change independent living for the elderly, fly a mini drone, and watch a 3D printer in action – all for free. It's criminally underrated.

» Don't leave without dragging your buddies to the Manga Generator photo booth to create a manga-likeness of you all.

PLAY MUSEUM

Map 6; Green Springs W3, 3-1 Midoricho, Tachikawa;
///rips.slurred.second; www.play2020.jp

Fun for kids and adults alike, this museum had locals talking before it even opened its doors in 2020. Spinning art into a playground, it allows you to touch and play with various installations. Exhibitions are divided into two camps: a permanent one celebrating a famous picture-book artist, and a rotating one focusing on various creators. But the fun doesn't stop at the exhibits: craft workshops invite you to create and then display your work in the gallery, sound workshops

Sample the café's themed food and drink menu, which changes to reflect every exhibition.

let you invent rhythms with handmade instruments, and the library is an escape from the havoc with more than 700 picture books to cosy up with.

SPACE MUSEUM TENQ

Map 3; Tokyo Dome City 6F, 1-3-61 Koraku, Bunkyo;
///dance.monopoly.family; www.tokyo-dome.co.jp

Seeing is believing at this futuristic science museum, where nine cool and educational displays aim to demystify the mysteries of space exploration. The biggest attraction is the dome-shaped Theater Sora, where you can gaze upon earth and space from above thanks to high-definition software. Itching to get hands-on? Head to the Imagination Room. Boffins try their smarts at creating their own planets, while kids get the answer to the important question: "what type of alien are you?"

TOSHIBA SCIENCE MUSEUM

Map 6; 72-34 Horikawa-cho, Saiwai, Kawasaki, Kanagawa;
///develops.bravest.blunt; www.toshiba-mirai-kagakukan.jp

It's a museum about Toshiba by Toshiba, so yes, you'd be forgiven for dismissing this as an exercise in self-congratulation. Put aside your cynicism and enter this computer-geek haven: it's free, interesting, and lets you try out new technology. Through interactive displays and live experiments, you'll learn about the company's history, technological developments, and future aspirations – and have fun doing so.

Pop Culture

Futuristic pop culture borders on an obsession in Tokyo. Japan's geeky cultural exports are entrenched in nearly every aspect of life, from cafés dedicated to cartoons to museums that recreate fantastical worlds.

TOEI ANIMATION MUSEUM
Map 6; 2-10-5 Higashioizumi, Nerima; ///setting.stone.mole; www.museum.toei-anim.co.jp

Though locals will admit they spend more time bingeing anime than trying to create their own franchise, this place at least gets the good intentions going. Founded by Toei, one of the world's biggest anime studios, this museum displays drawings, storyboards, and videos to show how animated scenes are created. Inspiration may well strike.

TV ASAHI
Map 5; 6-9-1 Roppongi, Minato; ///pops.tallest.tribes; www.tv-asahi.co.jp

Anime has TV Asahi to thank for creating some of its most loved characters – Doraemon, Kamen Rider, Crayon Shin-chan. When this famed network started producing anime series in the 1970s, it helped to popularize the genre around the world – and a little self-thanks is warranted at its headquarters, which acts like a shrine to its best exports. Parents relive memories at the changing exhibits while their kids pose next to giant statues with a newfound love for anime.

GHIBLI MUSEUM

Map 6; 1-1-83 Shimorenjaku, Mitaka; ///divider.ground.glass; www.ghibli-museum.jp

If *Spirited Away* had you feeling all kinds of whimsical, you're going to want to secure a ticket to this museum – months in advance, it's that popular. Put together like a film set, with winding staircases, tiny mystery doors, and towering character models, this attraction whisks you away to Studio Ghibli's universe. But it's not all fantastical: the mock animation room and the short movie screenings give budding filmmakers insider know-how on the creative process, too. It's all about immersing yourself in this world – photos aren't even allowed, so put your cameras away and escape for a few hours.

» Don't leave without visiting one of the whimsically decorated washrooms – they're a surprisingly pretty sight.

Try it!
CUPNOODLE CREATIONS

If (like the rest of the population) you've spent many days dependent on Japan's famous instant noodles, why not make your own unique blend inside Yokohama's Cupnoodles Museum *(www.cupnoodles-museum.jp)*?

Solo, Pair, Crowd

A day in Tokyo without some pop culture fun is unthinkable, but getting your obsession going is easy.

FLYING SOLO
Greet the stars

Detour to Nerima – known as the birthplace of Japanese animation – and make your way to Oizumi Anime Gate. Life-sized bronze statues of iconic characters like Astro Boy are the only company you'll need.

IN A PAIR
Oodles of noodles

Only in Tokyo would you find a museum dedicated to noodles. At the Shin-Yokohama Ramen Museum, sample your way through endless bowls from famous chains while you catch up with your bestie.

FOR A CROWD
Get your game face on

Nothing says teamwork like sailing a ghost ship or fighting monsters, and that's exactly what you get at VR theater TYFFONIUM Odaiba – just in a fantasy world, that is.

SNOOPY MUSEUM

Map 6; 3-1-1 Tsuruma, Machida; ///wake.inserted.spoiled;
www.snoopymuseum.tokyo

Though the *Peanuts* comic didn't originate in Japan, that doesn't stop locals obsessing over the beagle at its helm. Massive Snoopy statues and interviews with creator Charles M. Schulz are reason enough to visit this museum, but the interactive workshops are what keep families returning (because who doesn't want to design a Snoopy tote bag?).
» Don't leave without sampling something from the Snoopy-themed menu in the museum's popular Peanuts Cafe.

SUGINAMI ANIMATION MUSEUM

Map 6; 3-29-5 Suginami, Kamiogi; ///acute.tripped.playoffs; www.sam.or.jp

Home to over 130 studios, Suginami ward is the center of Japanese animation, and this hands-on museum lets you get in on the action. Fancy yourself a voice actor? Hit up the dubbing booth. More of an illustrator? Turn your drawings into film at the DIY animation studio.

SANRIO PUROLAND

Map 6; 1-31 Ochiai, Tama; ///miss.couches.spades;
www.en.puroland.jp

Travel to Tokyo and you can't miss Hello Kitty, plastered on everything from stationery to bullet trains. Though she may hog the limelight, this theme park lets you meet her friends, too. Avoid the parties of pre-teens that take over on the weekend and visit during the week, when it's blessedly quieter and those meet-and-greets last longer.

Culture Live

Much like the city at large, Tokyo's live circuit scene champions both old and new voices. Tradition lives on in the land of theater, while creative lectures and comedy gigs welcome modern entertainment.

PECHAKUCHA NIGHT

Various locations; www.pechakucha.org/cities/tokyo

Translating to "chit chat," Pechakucha is like a TED Talk in hyperspeed. Giving a fresh take on the public speaking scene, talks – held in both Japanese and English – are based on the 20x20 format: speakers have 20 slides and 20 seconds per slide to get their ideas across to an audience, all of whom come for a quick, powerful dose of inspiration. What started as a one-off event in Tokyo has become a global phenomenon, where designers, artists, and architects show their work to a relaxed community of fellow creatives.

KABUKIZA THEATRE

Map 5; 4-12-15 Ginza, Chuo; ///avid.pose.carrots; www.kabuki-za.co.jp

Despite having a high-brow feel to it (think well-dressed patrons and red carpets), there's no hint of exclusivity at Tokyo's principal theater for Kabuki. The classical Japanese dance-drama artform started life

Can't commit time and money to a four-hour show? Get a cheaper single-act *(makumi)* ticket at the door.

as a form of entertainment for the masses, and continues that legacy here thanks to cheap ticket options and a device that adds subtitles to performances.

TOKYO COMEDY BAR

Map 1; 3F, 1-5-9 Dogenzaka, Shibuya; ///bids.requests.valley; www.tokyocomedybar.com

Not only is this Tokyo's first stand-up comedy club, it's more importantly where the city's first roast battle event took place – a now regular English-friendly night that always sells out. While eight comedians go head-to-head in an attempt to outwit one another for the crown, audience members sip craft beer, thankful for not being in the firing line. This is not for the easily offended, nor is it one to rock up to unprepared: check the bar's socials for dates and buy your tickets fast.

» Don't leave without asking the staff about the comedy classes on offer – who knows, you could be the next comedian in a savage roast.

SUNTORY HALL

Map 5; 1-13-1 Akasaka, Minato; ///collide.deaf.puff; www.suntory.co.jp

Despite its prestige, this beautiful concert hall is dedicated to making world-class music accessible for all. The lunchtime organ recitals are free (after signing up), and a savior for yen-watching students with a penchant for orchestral music. Can't spare your lunch hour? Save a visit for local holidays and celebrations like Tanabata (Star Festival), when world-class performances are held.

Liked by the locals

"Pirates of Tokyo Bay is a perfect way to experience the heart and soul of Tokyo, laughing alongside locals. The improv comedy show is performed in both English and Japanese, so everyone can have fun."

MIKE STAFFA, PIRATES OF TOKYO BAY

PIRATES OF TOKYO BAY

Map 4; Roob 6 Bldg 4F, 1-13-3 Ebisunishi, Shibuya;
///sing.journals.website; www.piratesoftokyobay.com

The Pirates improv group proves that comedy (in the form of gibberish
and pantomime) can transcend language barriers. Want to feel fluent
in Japanese, bond with bilingual locals, and enjoy a good belly laugh
while doing it? Then book onto a monthly show before it sells out.

GLOBAL RING THEATRE

Map 6; 1-8-26 Nishiikebukuro, Toshima; ///coconut.split.singer;
www.globalring-theatre.com

Combining the cool vibe of open-air movies with a traditional theater
calendar and a stage, this outdoor theater venue has fast become
a staple for an eclectic crowd. Students come for the free tickets;
theater lovers for the live dance and classical shows, enhanced by the
immersive 360-degree sound and towering screen display.

» Don't leave without stocking up on snacks and drinks at the
nearby Global Ring Cafe before a performance.

KANZE NOGAKUDO

Map 5; Ginza Six B3F, 6-10-1 Ginza, Chuo;
///appeal.lamps.monitors; www.kanze.net

Specializing in the slow-moving, mask-wearing performance art of
Japanese Noh, this theater is an acquired taste. With pew-like seats
dotted with dapperly dressed, typically retired Ginza residents, the
people-watching is almost as exciting as what's happening on stage.

Sport Spectacles

Locals aren't raucous very often, but put on a match and passion hits a fever pitch. Ancient sports and Western imports are pillars of culture – though the sports tend to come second to the antics of the crowd.

RYOGOKU KOKUGIKAN

Map 3; 1-3-28 Yokoami, Sumida; ///strong.savers.neat; www.sumo.or.jp

It's this very stadium that gives the neighborhood of Ryogoku the nickname of "sumo town." The centerpiece of sumo culture, this is where the blockbuster battles of the season (that's January, May, and September) take place. Such is its reputation that locals go into a frenzy when tickets are released a month in advance, but all is not lost if you don't nab one. On match days, fans wait in line

Try it!
TRY SUMO THIS

Want to be more than a spectator? Sign up for the sumo experience at Raien *(www. raien.co)*, where former wrestlers teach you some tricks. Women are allowed to enter the sacred ring here, contrary to tradition.

outside the ticket office at 6am, when 400 same-day tickets are released (three hours later, mind you). Once you're inside, there's nothing quite like the gasps that fill the arena when the wrestlers collide with a crash.

KORAKUEN HALL

Map 3; 1-3-61 Korakuen, Bunkyo; ///fishery.reporter.responds; www.tokyo-dome.co.jp/hall

WWE may be the world's biggest pro wrestling brand, but Japan's own league, the NJPW (New Japan Pro Wrestling), always produces the most exciting matches. Feel the tension at Korakuen Hall build to breaking point as the nation's typically reserved citizens collectively lose their minds, hooting and hollering for their favorite stars. It's impossible not to get swept up in the theater of it all.

ARASHIO-BEYA SUMO STABLE

Map 3; 2-47-2 Nihonbashihamacho, Chuo; ///prongs.towers.stew; www.arashio.net

Being in town in the sumo offseason has its advantages. The main one? Seeing the wrestlers in action at "sumo stables," where they live and practice when tournaments aren't in session. Though many stables are members-only, Arashio-Beya bucks that trend. Between 7:30 and 10am you can catch high-energy morning practices, known as *asa-geiko*, up close through the streetside windows.

>> **Don't leave without** waiting outside once the daily practice is over; the wrestlers come out for pictures and to greet fans.

NIPPON BUDOKAN

Map 3; 2-3 Kitanomarukoen, Chiyoda; ///slamming.nappy.mistaken; www.nipponbudokan.or.jp

When it comes to martial arts, this venue is holy ground. Created to host the first ever judo event in the 1964 Olympics, Nippon Budokan single-handedly popularized the likes of karate, kendo, and *aikido*. Enthusiasts pack into what feels like a theater when tournaments are on, where dramatic silences from *kyudo* archers and war-like shouts from kendo swordsmen always result in a thrilling spectacle.

MEIJI JINGU STADIUM

Map 2; 3-1 Kasumigaokamachi, Shinjuku; ///examples.bulb.glides; www.jingu-stadium.com

It's hard to find a local who doesn't rave about the home ground of baseball legends the Yakult Swallows. Unbeknown to the fans who only filter in for games, however, are the free night yoga sessions held on the very same pitch. A Mexican wave of downward dogs replaces the cheers from spectactors when over 13,000 yogis don their exercise pants, grab a towel, and join a diverse crew under the stars.

RED BULL GAMING SPHERE TOKYO

Map 2; 3-33-18 Nakano, Nakano; ///sneezed.revives.prove; www.redbull.com

Lightning-fast thumbs, beads of sweat dripping from foreheads, and players narrowing in on their competition: after watching impressive feats of agility and strategy at Red Bull Gaming Sphere,

Compete with some of the best at the Red Bull Monday Night Streaks to win real cash prizes.

you'll never question whether esports are real sports again. Whether you're here to compete or watch others play the likes of FIFA, there's a real camaraderie to it all.

TOKYO DOME

Map 3; 1-3-61 Koraku, Bunkyo; ///probing.breath.pipes; www.tokyo-dome.co.jp

Synchronized chants, roaring cheers, wild towel waving: it's the crowd you'll be watching at this stadium, never mind the baseball game. Known for its carnival-like atmosphere, the home ground of the city's beloved Yomiuri Giants is all about the rivalry between the home fans and the away fans (or die-hard haters known as the anti-Giants). So, make a decision — are you home or away?

» Don't leave without visiting the Ball Park Store to buy merchandise to cheer with. Don't worry — it offers goods from 12 baseball teams.

JAPAN NATIONAL STADIUM

Map 2; 10-1 Kasumigaokamachi, Shinjuku; ///cheaper.mule.follow; (03) 3403 4150

Despite being postponed during the pandemic, the 2020 Olympics were a strong source of national pride for Tokyoites, even warranting a swanky new stadium. If anything makes up for not being able to cheer in the bleachers during the games, it's a free tour of the arena. Walk the track field, film yourself jumping over a hurdle, and see the Olympic torch up-close in this piece of city history.

MINAMI-
AOYAMA

*Hinokicho
Park*

AKASAKA

**Ponder the works at
THE NATIONAL ART
CENTER, TOKYO**
There's no permanent collection
at this massive center – just drop
in, mooch around the traveling
exhibitions, then visit the gift shop.

*Erected in 1954,
Kanaderu Otome –
a statue of a woman
playing a guitar by Shin
Hongo – is a symbol of
hope and peace.*

*Aoyama
Cemetery*

4

3

ROPPONGI

GAIEN

**Amble through
ROPPONGI TUNNEL**
Lining the walls of this
tunnel are five massive,
thought-provoking murals.
Venture in for some photo
ops – there's a giant zipper
and a bold seaside scene.

Perrotin *is the art
gallery known for
putting Japanese
contemporary artist
Takashi Murakami on
the world stage.*

ROPPONGI - DORI

EXPRESSWAY NO. 3

2

**Marvel at the
ROPPONGI HILLS
INSTALLATIONS**
This area is sprinkled with
cool outdoor art. Walk
under Louise Bourgeois'
"Maman" spider, then
check out Isa Genzken's
massive "Rose."

*Roppongi
Hills*

NISHI-
AZABU

1

**Look out for the
STREET
FURNITURE**
Keyakizaka Street is
full of public art that
doubles as chairs. Perch
on the likes of Jasper
Morrison's "Park Bench."

KEYAKI - ZAKA

MOTO-
AZABU

| 0 meters | 200 |
| 0 yards | 200 |

An afternoon's stroll through
arty Roppongi

Think Roppongi is just buzzing clubs and bars? The district is famed for its vibrant nightlife, but it's also one of Tokyo's major art hubs — there's even an annual Roppongi Art Night. As well as cutting-edge contemporary galleries (three of which are known as the Roppongi Art Triangle), this district is a literal canvas, peppered with public art sculptures and murals. Let the partygoers take over in the evening — days here are all about creative energy and soaking up artistic talent.

5

Get creative at a CALLIGRAPHY ART CLASS
In Japan, calligraphy is considered an art form. Sign up for an English-friendly class with master Yamamoto Kouga to learn some techniques.

ROPPONGI - DORI

SHI - DORI

ROPPONGI

1. Street Furniture
Around 6-15-1
Roppongi, Minato
///invent.outings.headline

2. Roppongi Hills Installations
6-4-1 Roppongi, Minato;
www.roppongihills.com
///bouncing.vitamins.scope

3. Roppongi Tunnel
Around 7-22
Roppongi, Minato
///tycoons.pity.building

4. The National Art Center, Tokyo
7-22-2 Roppongi, Minato;
www.nact.jp
///solve.helpers.voltage

5. Calligraphy Art Class
#408 Roppongi Heights,
4-1-16 Roppongi, Minato;
www.calligraphy-art.jp
///divide.escapes.wallet

Kanaderu Otome
///single.aimless.scary

Perrotin
///altering.language.grabs

AZABU-JUBAN

NIGHTLIFE

When the sun sets, Tokyo's streets buzz with a vibrancy that lasts into the early hours. Nights pass hopping between low-key taverns, frenetic clubs, and soothing bathhouses.

Top Yokocho

Navigating a traditional yokocho, or alleyway, is a post-work custom. Packed into these narrow streets are some of the best izakaya (gastropubs) and bars, where locals head to catch up and unwind.

SANKAKU CHITAI

Map 4; 2-15 Sangenjaya, Setagaya; ///less.clubs.arrives

Don't be nervous about entering what seems like this regulars-only, very local *yokocho*. Yes, this off-the-beaten-track alleyway is at the heart of the Sangenjaya neighborhood, where everyone seems to know everyone, but that gives it a friendly feel. Out-of-towners are most welcome at whatever spot they enter along the alley, be it a Japanese restaurant or an old-school tavern.

NONBEI YOKOCHO

Map 1; 1-25 Shibuya, Shibuya; ///guardian.sanded.allergy; www.nonbei.tokyo

With a nickname like "Drunkards' Alley," it's no surprise this stretch is all about drinking. But it's not your expected rowdy road – rather, locals settle into their favorite bar (there's 40 odd) and nurse a drink for a few hours. Most spaces only fit up to four or five patrons, making for

Head here in the afternoon to visit Takoyakido and enjoy a typical Japanese snack of takoyaki.

an intimate night where you can cosy up next to these regulars. If you visit the same bar again, you'll likely come across familiar faces – new friends, if you will.

HARMONICA YOKOCHO

Map 6; 1-1-1 Kichijoji Honcho, Musashino; ///blocking.dogs.punch

A sleepy maze of lanes by day, this *yokocho* comes alive at night when lanterns are lit, the smell of aromatic Chinese and Japanese dishes wafts down the alleyways, and distinctive chatter fills the air. Harmonica Yokocho holds onto its roots as a haunt for laborers and workers to convene after a long day (Kichijoji was once a working-class area), but has also made room for a younger, fresher crowd. Expect a mix of older, time-honored bars and modern *izakaya*, with a varied clientele to match.

» **Don't leave without** grabbing a plate of fresh sushi for dinner from popular Katakuchi, a tiny but amazing bar.

AMEYA-YOKOCHO

Map 3; 4-10 Ueno, Taito; ///property.audible.price

A postwar black market turned regular food market, Ameyoko (as it's known) still retains a shabby charm that is vanishing in the increasingly slick modern city. Nothing is prettified here, where a cluster of cheap, rugged *izakaya* lie beneath rattling train tracks. You probably won't be able to hear yourself speak over the vendors bartering, but that's okay – you'll be too busy tucking into yakitori chicken and *okonomiyaki*.

EBISU YOKOCHO

Map 4; 1-7-4 Ebisu, Shibuya; ///lion.asteroid.employ;
www.ebisu-yokocho.com

It can be hard to decide on a single venue when you're trawling a *yokocho* with various friends, but Ebisu doesn't let you settle for a spot you're not in the mood for. This indoor "alleyway" is a luxury, home to small micro-restaurants all under one roof. There's a food hall vibe to the proceedings: order fried noodles from one stall while your friends hit up a BBQ joint, then tuck in together at one of the many tables.

GOLDEN GAI

Map 2; 1-1-6 Kabukicho, Shinjuku; ///medium.spreads.void;
www.goldengai.jp

Okay, this is the big one, and it's world-famous for a reason. More than 200 tiny bars and restaurants jostle side-by-side in this labyrinth of six dark alleys and backlit acrylic signs. It's got a touristy reputation,

Shh!

Located just a block away from Ebisu Yokocho is Bar Odin, an old-school basement cocktail bar that offers a pretty fine selection of whisky and rare malts. Those who know about it trail in for a quieter drink after ambling through the nearby *yokocho*, before heading home for the night. The seasonal fruit cocktails on the menu are a must, as are the divine plates of pasta that pair well with any drink you order.

which many of the bars play on by adding a cover charge, but make no mistake – it's still a local favorite. You'll just have to look a bit harder to find the less crowded and more welcoming spots (you may get some side-eye from regular patrons if you fail to spot the "no tourists" or "regulars only" signs on some of the doors). Should you need a helping hand, start at Ace's, an English-friendly place where a mix of locals and tourists mingle, and then head to Death Match in Hell which, despite its name, is a warm and tiny bar that plays, you guessed it, a whole lot of metal music. Whatever you do, don't arrive too early, as nothing opens before 9pm.

» Don't leave without sipping on a freshly squeezed lemon sour at The Open Book – it's the only drink this book-lined bar makes.

OMOIDE YOKOCHO

Map 2; 1-2 Nishishinjuku, Shinjuku;
///precautions.outdoor.majority; www.shinjuku-omoide.com

You may not think much of a *yokocho* with a nickname like "Piss Alley," but rest assured the only thing you'll smell along this stretch is smoke from yakitori grills. Omoide's nickname comes from its origins as an illegal drinking den back in the 1940s, when a lack of restrooms resulted in – well, you can imagine. And the past certainly defines this *yokocho*; Omoide Yokocho literally translates to "Memory Lane," and though it was rebuilt in the late 20th century following a fire, it's managed to preserve an Old Tokyo vibe. Sure, it's not the most beautiful alley in the city, but that's why it typifies a retro Japanese feel. Unlike other *yokocho* which are mainly about the bars, Omoide Yokocho is a great place for eating with a side of people-watching.

Favorite Izakaya

Ah, the Japanese gastropub: the hub of social life come night. Ordering a few dishes to share with friends at these down-to-earth joints (typically found in yokocho*) is an integral custom in Tokyo.*

RYUKYU CHINESE TAMA

Map 1; 2-3-2 Shibuya, Shibuya; ///commented.privately.highways; www.tama2007.jp

Always packed out with Aoyama's young professionals, this *izakaya* feels like being at a friend's dinner-turned-house party. Infectious laughter fills the air until midnight, and mates come for the vibrant ambience as much as the Okinawan cuisine. The chef is always up for a chat, so nab a table by the open kitchen (the best seats in the house) and get talking while you tuck into taco rice.

UOSHIN NOGIZAKA

Map 5; 9-6-32 Akasaka, Minato; ///marathon.offline.parts; www.uoshins.com

Giving off the ambience of a beer garden, this place ticks all the boxes for a classic post-work hangout: a lively atmosphere, affordable quality seafood, and great beer. It's a boisterous spot when evening rolls around and groups of business workers trickle in after a long day, but it's not intimidating thanks to its down-to-earth vibe, with diners chilling out on beer crates around haphazardly arranged tables.

» Don't leave without ordering the *nokkezushi* – cucumber *maki* rolls topped with fresh *uni* (sea urchin), *ikura* (salmon roe), and crab.

IZAKAYA MASAKA
Map 1; Shibuya Parco B1F, Udagawacho, Shibuya;
///heat.crowd.teachers; www.masaka.ninja

In a city where nearly all *izakaya* cater to meat eaters, this rare vegan-friendly gem is a blessing. It may be located in Chaos Kitchen (also known as Shibuya Parco's basement food hall), but there's nothing chaotic about it. Appealing to tradition, it's a humble retreat with space for just 20 diners, designed to look and feel like an old-school *izakaya*. Regulars are evangelical about the mock chicken *karaage* – so much like the real thing that you might want to consult the chef.

Shh!

Tucked down a side street, 35 Steps Bistro in Shibuya (*www.raku-co.com*) takes its name from the exact amount of stairs you'll walk down to get from the building's front door to this basement bar. Once inside, lively parties of friends tuck into generous portions of affordable seafood, chatting loudly while chefs cook up feasts at the open counter. You can't go wrong ordering anything that's been grilled.

TATEMICHIYA

Map 4; 30-8 Sarugakucho, Shibuya; ///washed.else.uniform; (03) 5459-3431

In true rock 'n' roll style, only an in-crowd of cool kids know where to find this basement den, otherwise known as "Punk Rock Izakaya." It has the atmosphere of a secret afterparty: you enter a poster-decked room through a nondescript entrance, Japanese punk plays through the speakers, and the affable owner grills yakitori skewers while bantering with the regulars at the bar.

UOHARU

Map 5; Shin-Tokyo Bldg B1F, 3-3-1 Marunouchi, Chiyoda; ///aviation.gent.knee; (03) 6269-9099

The Tokyo food scene is known for the impeccable presentation of dishes, so much so that if ingredients are deemed imperfect, they're thrown out without a second thought. This sustainability-focused spot is on a mission to change this, serving up imperfect, but still very much edible, seafood from Tokyo's fish markets. And locals are all for it: friends gather here at night for catch-ups and a side portion of smugness, tucking into top-quality seafood at a reasonable price.

LANTERNE

Map 4; 3-1-11 Higashiyama, Meguro; ///writing.beside.pumpkin; www.lanterne.jp

High energy defines this ever-bustling spot, where nights are set to the buzz of animated chatter and glasses clinking. One of the more modern *izakaya* joints in town, this hip and stylish spot attracts, well,

Arrive for happy hour at 5pm, when you can get a drink and chicken *karaage* for just ¥100 until 7pm.

the hip and stylish. With a big communal table in the center, Lanterne is perfect for group hangouts, with enough space for all the food and local sake you'll order.

SHIRUBEE

Map 4; 2-18-2 Kitazawa, Setagaya;
///pumpkin.vipers.nuggets; (03) 3413-3785

From the outside, this backstreet *izakaya* looks like one of the area's more traditional establishments – and to an extent, it is. But like the area in which it resides, it's not afraid to blend classic with contemporary, and that means creative spins on Japanese dishes like cheese tofu with honey and salted squid guts. Rammed on weekends with rowdy groups enjoying life, it's a friendly, unpretentious, and exciting place to be.

» Don't leave without ordering the *shime saba* (seasoned mackerel) and witnessing the staff torch it at your table. It's a real show.

KUSHIWAKAMARU

Map 4; 1-19-2 Kamimeguro, Meguro; ///onto.unit.blaring;
(03) 3715-9292

The aroma of fresh-off-the-grill yakitori chicken hits you before you even enter Kushiwakamaru. Brimming with regulars getting their meat-on-a-stick fix, this no-frills spot makes for a convivial and pretty cheap night out. You'll leave smelling of smoke from the grills, but that's an old-school *izakaya* for you.

Music Nights

Frenetic pop fans and laidback jazz lovers plan their nights around music. Watching a band you've never heard of perform or listening to an eclectic set in a DJ bar makes up the heart and soul of the scene.

SANKEY'S PENTHOUSE

Map 1; Q Plaza Harajuku 10-11F, 6-28-6 Jingumae, Shibuya;
///trick.assures.orchestra; www.sankeyspenthouse.com

Sitting on the top floor of a department store, this swanky music lounge blends sophistication with a dash of late-night naughtiness. It's the place to see and be seen, where fashionable folk (Harajuku is the home of Tokyo's fashion industry, after all) come to recline on plush seating. Providing the soundtrack to their VIP-esque nights is a DJ set playing out techno and house tunes.

RUBY ROOM

Map 1; 2-25-17 Dogenzaka, Shibuya; ///cactus.smoking.curated;
www.rubyroomtokyo.com

This beloved venue has long been a lifeline for the city's indie music community, but that's not to say the programming is predictable. One evening a host of Weezer cover bands take over the small corner

The weekly open mic night is a bit of an institution. Visit on a Tuesday to see local artists do their thing.

stage; the next, a head-banging hotbox of heavy metal plays out. As long as you enter with no expectations (apart from to have fun), this venue never lets you down.

AKB48 THEATER

Map 3; 4-3-3 Sotokanda, Chiyoda; ///hobby.kick.advising; www.akb48.co.jp

When it comes to most J-Pop groups, waiting to see them perform at a yearly concert is often the norm. Not so for girl group AKB48 and their custom-made venue, where rotating members (there's been over 120 at a time) perform near-daily. Given how popular they've become, tickets are highly sought-after and awarded by a lottery system after applying via the website. It's a game of chance, but try your luck anyway: it's a lot of fun singing along with excitable fans.

» Don't leave without browsing the gift store, where you'll find a staggering array of AKB48-branded merch.

WWW

Map 1; 13-7 Udagawacho, Shibuya; ///reversed.able.oasis; www.www-shibuya.jp

For a crash course in the hottest new act in town, look no further than WWW. Budding critics and music aficionados pack out the rows here to catch the local "it" bands in the hope of bragging rights when they become the next international star. An impeccable sound system, stylishly bare interior, and chilled crowds make WWW the discerning indie music fan's favorite haunt.

NANAHARI

Map 3; Oriental Bldg, 2-7-1 Shinkawa, Chuo;
///shaped.usages.denote; www.ftftftf.com

This is the type of place you first visit because you know someone who's playing, and continue visiting because you've fallen in love with the venue. Nanahari books acts with no real rhyme or reason: avant-garde noise, spoken word, delicate folk, indie pop. Essentially, if the owner digs your sound, then you'll get on. Simply rock up with a few cans (you can BYO) and let Tokyo entertain you.

ZUBAR

Map 1; 1-6-3 Dogenzaka, Shibuya; ///trickle.football.boats; www.zubar.jp

There's something effortlessly cool about this underground venue, where tables come in the form of repurposed oil drums and the shelves look like reconfigured wooden pallets. Edgy cohorts float around the tiny dancefloor to eclectic DJ sets from local and renowned DJs, only taking a break to feast on Taiwanese cuisine served up here – surprisingly the perfect accompaniment to the spicy, unpredictable soundtrack.

BLUE NOTE TOKYO

Map 1; Raika Bldg, 6-3-16 Minamiaoyama, Minato;
///jiffy.swanky.awoken; www.bluenote.co.jp

Tokyo is a city infatuated with jazz music, and locals make their obsession clear at Blue Note: the city's most coveted jazz bar, where an empty seat is unheard of. Upscale sophistication defines this moody, low-lit space and the well-dressed patrons who sway to some of the most renowned local and international artists. Ticket prices come at a premium, but it's worth it for a night at this magical venue.

» Don't leave without inspecting the bar's original cocktail menu, which features drinks inspired by some of music's greats.

SHIMOKITAZAWA THREE
Map 4; B1F, 5-18-1 Kitazawa, Setagaya; ///secrets.kick.scanner; www.toos.co.jp/3

The energetic, creative spirit that defines Shimokitazawa lives strong in this basement den. Caring more about inducing moshpit mayhem than making money, it holds around 10 free events a month (check its social pages for a heads-up) to let bands of all genres reach new audiences. You'll end up spending the money you save on the entrance fee on multiple visits to the bar, as half your drinks will end up on the floor thanks to crowd-surfing guitarists. But who's complaining?

Just off Shimokitazawa's more central paths, 440 (Four Forty) *(SY Bldg 1F, 5-29-15 Daizawa, Setagaya)* is an unassuming bar and live music venue that hosts a diverse roster of acts. Often you'll find suited-up office workers sitting solo, focused on their favorite act performing, or friends supporting their friends as they brave the stage. The crowd here is notoriously so polite you can almost hear the ice melt in your lemon sour.

Cool Clubs

It's hard to believe that until 2015, Japan officially had a "no dancing" law. Locals make up for all that lost time today: missing the last train is intentional when it means letting loose into the early hours.

AISOTOPE LOUNGE

Map 2; 2-12-16 Shinjuku, Shinjuku; ///insiders.dozen.publish; www.aisotope-lounge.net

This stylish spot is well known by the area's locals as the place to catch big international queer and drag acts, who pop by for the venue's monthly parties. Marked on the calendar of every regular is the last weekend of October, when this club becomes the unofficial home of Tokyo's gay Halloween and hosts the most raunchy cosplay convention.

OATH

Map 1; Tosei Bldg B1F, 1-6-5 Dogenzaka, Shibuya; ///finger.describe.troubled; (03) 3461-1225

There's partying into the morning at a Tokyo club, and then there's partying at OATH. When the other clubs have closed and the first trains beckon bed time, the city's hardcore ravers choose to continue the night here, where local and international DJs keep the dancing going under antique chandeliers until 8am. It gives off major after-party vibes, with a basement location, low drink prices, and a friendly crowd. Bonus: unlike most clubs which are only open on weekends, this spot hosts events throughout the week, too.

AOYAMA HACHI

Map 1; Aoyama Bldg 2F-4F, 4-5-9 Shibuya; ///removes.climber.wings; www.aoyama-hachi.net

This long-standingShibuya party house has multiple rooms, each as hedonistic as the next. Travel through the four-storey space and you'll meet EDM heads moving to monotonous beats, B-boys busting moves to hip-hop, and hardcore music lovers banging their heads to rock, all in harmony under one roof. Whatever you're into, you're bound to find your people on the dancefloor.

» Don't leave without taking a break from the crowded rooms to enjoy the beautiful view over Roppongi from the second floor.

HARLEM

Map 1; Dr Jeekahn's Bldg 2F-3F, 2-4 Maruyamacho, Shibuya; ///sizes.reapply.notched; www.harlem.co.jp

Since opening in 1997, Harlem has been considered the "holy land" of hip-hop in Japan. It's always brimming with fly Tokyoites decked out in the latest streetwear staples, showing off their best dance moves (breakdancing is a regular sight) while local DJs and up-and-coming MCs spin rap and R&B tunes. Parties are held regularly, as are special events that draw international crowds.

BONOBO

Map 2; 2-23-4 Jingumae, Shibuya; ///droplet.inched.aviation;
www.bonobo.jp

A visit to Bonobo is the closest thing you'll find to a house party in Tokyo (it's more of a dinner party type of city). This quirky underground club and bar takes up space in an old two-storey house, complete with a rooftop terrace for chats under the stars. On the ground floor, a small crowd two-step to electronic and house music, dashing off to the bar for refreshments between songs. Above them, those who've danced a little too hard relax in a laidback lounge area – heck, it's even kitted out with traditional tatami mats and floor seating, so you can make yourself right at home. And, like any good house party, you're just as likely to meet a student handing out shots to everyone as you are newbies to the city determined to tell you their life story.

» Don't leave without checking out the website for upcoming music events and workshops, which tend to take place on the second floor.

ARTY FARTY

Map 2; 2-11-7 Shinjuku, Shinjuku; ///darling.ashes.oils;
(03) 5362-9720

A tongue-in-cheek name for a gay club that doesn't take itself too seriously, Arty Farty is a renowned spot where partiers come to thrash around to frenetic remixes of the day's hottest chart hits. With sticky floors, the sickly sweet smell of spirits and Red Bull in the air, and crowds packed onto a tiny dancefloor, it's a place for no-inhibitions dancing, forgotten conversations, and flirting over

Your entrance fee for Arty Farty gives you free access to its nearby sister club, The Annex.

a drink. It's welcome to all, but bear in mind that if you're visiting on a weekend, women can only enter with a male companion in tow.

NEW SAZAE

Map 2; 2F 2-18-5 Shinjuku, Shinjuku; ///goods.retire.snooze; (03) 6384-1978

A living, breathing, glittering time capsule, New Sazae overflows with retro ambience. Tokyo's oldest gay bar still in existence, it opened its doors in 1966 and has been providing a soundtrack of disco for Tokyo's LGBTQ+ community ever since. A local favorite in the city's gay quarter, this intimate and inclusive bar may not be particularly slick or fancy, but it's a piece of queer Tokyo history (there are fading photos of some of the bar's early patrons on the walls) and an excellent place to lose a Saturday night.

WOMB

Map 1; 2-16 Maruyamacho, Shibuya; ///spoon.approach.limo; www.womb.co.jp

It's a party almost every night at this subterranean music den, the throbbing heart of Shibuya's clubbing scene. Depending on the evening, music obsessives from all clubbing subcultures (J-pop, drum and bass, afro tech, to name a few) pack out the four-level space, dancing under the strobe lights while world-class DJs play. If it all gets too sweaty, take a break at the somewhat unexpected juice bar on the second floor.

Late-Night Bathing

Evenings in Tokyo are not all high-energy. Late-night soaks in public bathhouses have become a ritual to purify the body and relax the mind after a long day – just be sure to follow the rules (p11).

THERMAE-YU

Map 2; 1-1-2 Kabukicho, Shinjuku; ///edit.chase.perfume;
www.thermae-yu.jp

This six-story *onsen* (hot-spring bath) may be home to an impressive amount of tubs, but regulars have only one area in mind when night draws in: the main bath. Known as a *rotenburo*, Thermae-Yu's outdoor bath perfectly balances the high heat of the water – brought daily from Nakaizu – with a breeze of Tokyo's cooler air. Nothing says tonic for the soul quite like stargazing while bathing.

RYOGOKU EDO-YU

Map 3; 1-5-8 Kamezawa, Sumida; ///puzzled.novel.tight;
www.edoyu.com/ryougoku

Blurring the lines between a luxury spa and traditional bathhouse, this *sento* (man-made bath) is the kind of place that you pop into for an afternoon soak and before you know it, you're making a night of it.

Start with a dip in the soothing herbal tub, head to the restaurant for dinner, and then settle into a reclining chair in the chill-out area to, well, chill out. If you nod off, you'll be happy to know it stays open until 9am (when it closes for two hours, before opening again).

SPA LAQUA

Map 3; 1-1-1 Kasuga, Bunkyo; ///doctors.bumping.retract; www.laqua.jp/spa

While thrillseeker friends take to the roller coasters at the Tokyo Dome City complex outside, those in the group that prefer a slower pace of life relax at this luxury *onsen*. Nicknamed "beauty spring," Spa LaQua is known for its sodium-chloride-enriched water, which aids metabolism and skin health – and frankly soothes the mind. So whether you prefer to get your kicks from the theme park adrenaline rush or a Thai massage while looking out at Tokyo's twinkling city, you'll feel revitalized.

>> **Don't leave without** getting a rejuvenating Korean body scrub to ensure your skin is primed to take in all the minerals from the water.

Try it!
BUILD YOUR OWN BATH

Want to run a mineral-rich bath at home? The spa Take no Yu *(1-9-13 Sekibara, Adachi)* – known as "Black Beauty Waters" – lets you buy some of its dark water with alleged beautifying properties for ¥20 per liter bottle.

DAIKOKU-YU

Map 2; 3-24-5 Nishihara, Shibuya; ///roofer.became.alleges; (03) 3485-1701

Tucked down the back of an outdoor coin laundry, this neighborhood joint retains an old-town public-bath atmosphere in everything from the decor to the patrons. Bathhouses have always functioned like community centers (nothing says intimacy like bathing with your neighbors), but this tradition can get overlooked in modern spots. Not so here, where wellness is about more than just mineral water and regulars come by primarily to socialize after a long day.

BUNKA YOKUSEN

Map 4; 3-6-8 Higashiyama, Meguro;
///busters.maternal.stocks; www.bunkayokusen1010.com

Ikejiri-Ohashi is a cool pocket of the city, and the crowd that frequents Bunka Yokusen at night is no different. Renovated by Kentaro Imai, an architect who gives old bathhouses a second lease of life, this indoor *sento* has a modern edge that draws in younger folk – some of whom were skeptical about communal bathing before visiting. A jazz soundtrack and a tattoos-welcome policy help matters, too.

NATURAL HOT SPRING HEIWAJIMA

Map 6; 2F Big Fun Heiwajima, 1-1-1 Heiwajima, Ota;
///interval.dame.think; www.heiwajima-onsen.jp

Got an early morning flight and refuse to splurge on an extra night at your hotel? Put your remaining yen toward this natural hot spring complex, a 15-minute drive from Haneda Airport and open until 8am.

Don't book a taxi to Haneda Airport – this complex offers a free shuttle bus service every morning.

Spend some time in the sauna and hot springs before relaxing in the spacious lounge areas – your body will thank you on that long-haul flight.

TOGOSHI GINZA ONSEN

Map 4; 2-1-6 Togoshi, Shinagawa; ///lookout.secondly.caves; www.togoshiginzaonsen.com

It's not easy to find a bathhouse that allows tattoos (they were once considered a symbol of crime in Japan and subsequently banned), but this spot bends that tradition while still maintaining an old-school vibe. Sure, it's sleek and stylish in design, but it offers the likes of authentic hot-spring water and a typical electric bath (it's safe, don't worry). It's a firm favorite with an inked-up international crowd who come for the relaxed attitude.

» Don't leave without buying a glass bottle of milk from the changing room vending machine. A little post-bath dairy is a Japanese tradition.

HACHIMAN-YU

Map 2; 1-2-10 Tomigaya, Shibuya; ///pens.asteroid.enhances; (03) 3468-0337

If you visit this simple, affordable neighborhood bath often enough on week nights, you'll begin to recognize the regulars who unwind after work or freshen up after a running session in nearby Yoyogi Park (p168). The electric bath is the perfect treat for stiff muscles from all that circuit training – or simply a long day spent sightseeing.

Game Night

When friends find a way of gathering after too long apart, they opt for a night of gaming sessions and sporty activities. It's a chance to unwind, indulge in healthy competition and fuel childhood nostalgia.

GAME BAR A-BUTTON

Map 3; 1-13-9 Taito, Taito; ///pebbles.laying.wire; www.a-button.jp

Entering this tiny arcade bar feels a lot like intruding upon someone's personal gaming den. Brimming with paraphernalia, toys, and retro consoles from the owner's collection, Game Bar A-Button takes you on a serious nostalgia trip. Located in the heart of Tokyo's main geek district, Akihabara, it's where hardcore gamers and tech developers (including some big names in the gaming industry) come to bond over a game of Atari or Mario Cart while chugging down a craft beer.

TAKKYU SAKABA PONZO

Map 1; 12-7 Udagawacho, Shibuya; ///qualify.snapped.jazz;
www.ponzo.jp

This shabby gaming *izakaya* – a rare find in Tokyo – always seems to make its way into post-work Friday-night plans. Evenings here are set to the soundtrack of ping pong balls flying on and off the tables in the corner, where competitive groups get louder by the hour, fueled by all-you-can-drink cocktails. In the main area, quieter twosomes share pizza over a board game on the low tables and suited colleagues play a round of darts with a glass of sake.

JOYPOLIS

Map 5; DECKS Tokyo Beach 3F-5F, 1-6-1 Daiba, Minato; ///oils.response.diagram; www.tokyo-joypolis.com

By day, families take over gaming giant Sega's indoor amusement park, where thrilling rides and virtual reality (VR) attractions await. But after dark, those excited shrieks from the kids are swapped out with the sounds of adults running riot in this grown-ups' playground. Dating duos fight zombies in frightening games of laser tag while groups of mates revisit the beloved video games of their childhoods.

» Don't leave without looking out for the *purikura* photo booths to take a big-eyed *kawaii* shot like Tokyo's teens.

OSLO BATTING CENTER

Map 2; 2-34-5 Kabukicho, Shinjuku; ///dots.storage.water; www.oslo.ecweb.jp

Surrounded by adult entertainment venues, clubs, and dive bars, this automated batting center is one of the more tasteful late-night establishments in the heart of nightlife district Kabukicho. It's high-energy come evening, when families are replaced by baseball-loving businessmen, the thwack of balls being hit a sure sign of letting off steam. Serious baseball players need not apply.

Solo, Pair, Crowd

Tokyo is a playground for those who are young at heart, with endless ways to relieve daily stresses.

FLYING SOLO
Game on
A laid-back night of playing video games and meeting new friends is guaranteed at Tokyo Video Gamers in Akihabara. Better yet, games are free to play.

IN A PAIR
Beat the boredom
For a chilled evening, bring a friend and your competitive spirit to the cosy café and bar Glück in Iidabashi, where cocktails are plentiful and the German-imported board and card games even more so.

FOR A CROWD
Sing for your supper
If anything will tempt your mates to belt out classic tunes, it's a video games-inspired karaoke venue. At Akihabara's Pasela Resorts, each room is garishly decked out (try to nab the Final Fantasy-themed space).

SASAZUKA BOWL

Map 2; 3/4F, 1-57-10 Sasazuka, Shibuya; ///lookout.alarm.vase; www.sasazukabowl.com

Nobody can quite pinpoint when this neighborhood bowling alley went from gritty family attraction to retro-cool hub, but it probably had something to do with the album launch party held here by Daft Punk back in 2013. This party vibe shows no signs of slowing, either, with Friday and Saturday nights giving cool kids and serious bowlers alike a chance to let loose to great DJ sets and competitive late-night sessions – booze optional. If you have the stamina, take up one of the all-you-can-bowl deals and keep going until 5am.

» Don't leave without exploring the store for some one-of-a-kind merch. Sasazuka Bowl tote bag, anyone?

KARAOKE KAN

Map 1; 30-8 Udagawacho, Shibuya; ///stump.magnetic.retail; www.karaokekan.jp

Thanks to its role in the film *Lost in Translation*, this once generic branch of the Karaoke Kan chain has become the poster child of the Japanese karaoke experience for the Western world. That doesn't make it any less of a local favorite, though. Karaoke, which originates in Japan, is a nightly pastime in Tokyo, and this simple joint bustles with both giggling students and suit-clad businessmen looking to unwind. The interior mirrors Karaoke Kan's other outposts, but film fans get a kick knowing this is "the one from the movie." Challenge your mate to a sing-off and belt your heart out to a track from the Spice Girls and other 1990s songs you loved as a teen.

An evening out in
buzzing Shinjuku

There's a nightlife district for every taste in Tokyo
– Roppongi's foreigner-friendly dance clubs,
Ginza's classy bars, Shibuya's youthful energy – but
Shinjuku has all this and more. It comes alive at
night (neon literally lights up the streets), when
locals navigate the labyrinthian lanes lined
with cheap *izakaya*, raucous clubs, and vibrant
karaoke dens. Follow suit and blow off some
steam at the end of the day. If you're not careful,
an evening in Shinjuku can fast turn into the
morning (as it should).

1. Shinjuku Central Park
2-11 Nishishinjuku; www.city.
shinjuku.lg.jp/seikatsu
///slicing.solves.oldest

2. Omoide Yokocho
1-2 Nishishinjuku;
www.shinjuku-omoide.com
///precautions.outdoor.
majority

3. Karaoke Kan
1-5-7 Kabukicho;
www.karaokekan.jp
///plug.books.reshape

4. Golden Gai
1-1-6 Kabukicho;
www.goldengai.jp
///medium.spreads.void

5. Thermae-Yu
1-1-2 Kabukicho;
www.thermae-yu.jp
///edit.chase.perfume

📍 **Tokyo Metropolitan
Government Building**
///magazine.nearing.
headache

**Watch the sunset at
SHINJUKU
CENTRAL PARK**
Nestled between many
skyscrapers, this understated
suburban park is rarely
crowded. Perch on the
grass and admire the skyline
as day turns into night.

*The north observation
deck at the* **Tokyo
Metropolitan
Government Building**
*offers a panoramic view
of the city until 11pm.*

Unwind at THERMAE-YU

Open 24 hours, this slick *onsen (p152)* is perfect for relaxing tired legs and minds. Soak away the day in the popular outdoor bath.

Dinner at OMOIDE YOKOCHO

Head to this retro, food-centric alleyway *(p139)* for a broad selection of fast Japanese cuisine, from yakitori to ramen.

2

3

4

5

Grab the mic at KARAOKE KAN

Get amped up belting out some classic tunes at this popular chain. It's housed in a high tower, so you can soak up incredible views too.

Enjoy a drink at GOLDEN GAI

Amble through this *yokocho (p138)*, glancing through little doorways and up stairways to find a bar to your liking.

Shinjuku's **Ni-chome** *district is home to some of the city's oldest clubs and the highest concentration of gay bars in the world.*

KITA-SHINJUKU

HYAKUNINCHO

OKUBO

NISHI-SHINJUKU

KABUKICHO

YAKUSINI DORI

MEIJI - DORI

SHINJUKU

KAIDO

CHUO - DORI

FUREAI - DORI

NISHI-SHINJUKU

KOSHU - KAIDO - DORI

Shinjuku Station

MEIJI - DORI

YOYOGI

SENDAGAYA

Shinjuku Gyoen Garden

| 0 meters | 300 |
| 0 yards | 300 |

OUTDOORS

Given Japan's Shinto belief in celebrating nature, locals cherish the great outdoors – admiring the cherry blossoms, exercising on the water, finding respite at shrines.

Tranquil Gardens

Embracing the ideologies of imperfect perfection and the fleetingness of nature, Tokyo's manicured gardens are where high-rise-apartment-bound locals head to appreciate the seasons and get back to nature.

INSTITUTE FOR NATURE STUDY

Map 4; enter at 5-21-5 Shirokanedai, Minato;
///elects.comet.fades; www.ins.kahaku.go.jp

Completely disproving any impression of Tokyo as a concrete jungle is this dense forest, a welcome surprise in bustling Minato. Here, the hurried steps of urbanites are drowned out by crows cawing. Few folk seem to know about it outside of the green-fingered members of the adjoining National Museum of Nature and Science, who use the grounds for research, and the plant lovers and birdwatchers who visit.

IMPERIAL PALACE EAST GARDENS

Map 3; enter at Ote-mon gate, 1-1 Chiyoda, Chiyoda;
///shifting.fear.dips; www.kunaicho.go.jp

Once home to one of the most powerful castles in the land, these gardens are now the stomping ground of the city's lycra-clad fitness fanatics, who use it as a running track. Sure, there's a lot of history here, with original moats, massive stones, and the walls of the former castle, but locals come for a morning run to soak up the pretty pond, lovely woodland area, and seasonal blooms — all in the shadow of the current royal family's lavish domestic home.

RIKUGIEN GARDENS

Map 3; enter at the eastern corner, 6-16-3 Honkomagome, Bunkyo;
///flatten.incoming.second; www.tokyo-park.or.jp

Rikugien was made for a wander — literally, it's a Japanese strolling garden. Created to be admired from every angle, these traditional Edo-era gardens (of which Rikugien is the finest) are all about the journey rather than the destination. At this garden, the impeccable design recreates landscapes from poems in miniature and the view changes with every few steps you take. Like an open-top biodome, its ability to block out the energy of the city makes it a respite for those seeking some natural healing.

>> **Don't leave without** seeing the weeping cherry blossom tree if you're visiting during the spring. It's beautifully lit up in the evening.

Try it!
BUILD A BONSAI

Feeling inspired after exploring the city's artfully manicured gardens? Take a bonsai class at Kunio Kobayashi's Bonsai School (*www.kunio-kobayashi.com*) to create your own little slice of Tokyo greenery.

MEGURO SKY GARDEN

**Map 4; 1-9-2 Ohashi, Meguro; ///rating.frantic.inhales;
www.city.meguro.tokyo.jp**

Located between residential blocks, suspended over a highway, and with an inconspicuous access point via a library, this rooftop garden couldn't be more well hidden. But it's become a staple in the lives of apartment-dwelling locals living nearby: owners walk their pooches, couples watch the sun set, and – rumor has it – there's a vine planted here that people use to make wine.

SHINJUKU GYOEN NATIONAL GARDEN

**Map 2; enter at Shinjuku gate, 11 Naitomachi, Shinjuku;
///informed.helm.powerful; www.env.go.jp**

Let the cherry blossom fanatics take over this garden with picnics in the spring: the fall is where it's at. As soon as the maple trees turn red in the Japanese garden, and a golden hue takes over the British

Shh!

Hidden inside the bamboo-lined and glossy black walls of the Nezu Museum (www.nezu-muse.or.jp) lies an unlikely garden. It was designed in the Japanese landscape style known as *shinzan-yukoku*, an aesthetic that pays tribute to nature's deep mountains and mysterious valleys. Home to a teahouse, stepping stone paths, and deep black ponds populated by golden koi, it's the epitome of an urban oasis.

garden, a calm descends. Leaf-peepers wrap up to embark on crisp strolls, where the only sounds are of leaves crunching beneath their feet and kids rolling on the fallen yellow foliage.

HAMARIKYU GARDENS

Map 5; enter at Shiodome Toll gate; 1-1 Hamarikyuteien, Chuo; ///rinses.recently.moss; www.tokyo-park.or.jp

Calling Hamarikyu an oasis would be a cliché if it didn't perfectly summarize the garden's ambience. Backdropped by gray towers that reflect off the central pond's still water, it's populated mostly by watercolor-painting aficionados. Come armed with your own sketchbook and brushes after exploring the high-speed streets of the neighboring Roppongi area and you'll fit right in.

» **Don't leave without** nibbling on Japanese sweets in the Nakajima no Ochaya teahouse – its views over the park are incomparable.

MEJIRO GARDEN

Map 2; 3-20-18 Mejiro, Toshima; ///central.hotdog.mystery; www.seibu-la.co.jp/mejiro-garden

The suburban incarnation of the city's more well-known green retreats, this spot has long been a staple for those who live in the neighborhood. The pretty setting, complete with a large pond and blooming flowers, is enough to draw retirees and nearby office workers here everyday, who set up stations on the benches with bento boxes in tow. The locals are always welcoming, so expect to exchange pleasantries while you tuck into your lunch.

Social Parks

As far as locals are concerned, Tokyo's parks are communal backyards where anything goes. Leisure time is spent on sprawling lawns: hanging out with pals, practicing a hobby, or simply lazing away.

INOKASHIRA PARK

Map 6; enter near Inokashira-koen station;
///football.blanked.sued; (03) 422-47-6900

Year after year, Tokyoites rank Kichijoji as one of the most desirable areas to live – thanks in large part to this luscious park, which acts as a microcosm of the friendly neighborhood. Walk through on a weekend and you'll see families setting up picnics after visiting the whimsical Ghibli Museum *(p121)* nearby, friends boating on Inokashira Pond, and local street artists displaying their work.

YOYOGI PARK

Map 2; enter near Harajuku station, 2-1 Yoyogikamizonocho,
Shibuya; ///living.hounded.echo; www.tokyo-park.or.jp

Central Tokyo's backyard, Yoyogi Park is most famous for its cherry blossom picnic parties and proximity to Meiji Shrine *(p177)*, but one visit here and you'll realize the biggest draw is the people-watching.

Rockabillies performing choreographed routines, impromptu music jam sessions, martial arts rehearsals, endless parades of pampered poodles: it's nothing short of a variety show, proudly brought to you by the colorful characters of Tokyo.

ODAIBA MARINE PARK

Map 5; 1-4 Odaiba, Minato; ///thorax.often.panther; www.tptc.co.jp/park
Who knew a reclaimed garbage dump could be so idyllic? Adjoining an artificial bay, this popular park is the sunset-watching spot of choice for groups of teenagers, photographers, and loved-up couples, given the New York City-esque landscape it overlooks. Witnessing the sun vanish behind the city's futuristic skyscrapers and the iconic Rainbow Bridge never gets old.

» Don't leave without looking out for Odaiba's very own Statue of Liberty, talking of New York City. It looks almost identical to its big sister (if you ignore the fact that it's a fraction of the size).

Shh!

In the quiet area of Meguro, between Toritsudaigaku and Gakugeidaigaku, lies the city's own suburban bamboo "forest," Suzume no Oyado Ryokuchi *(3-11-22 Himonya)*. It's typically tourist-free, given how small and out-of-the-way it is. Plan a BFF catch-up here and embark on a leisurely stroll through the 200-year-old compact bamboo grove. You'll pass friends playing frisbee and children seeking out insects.

KINUTA PARK

Map 6; 1-1 Kinutakoen, Setagaya; ///uproot.connects.parks;
(03) 3700-0414

You won't find many tourists in this neighborhood park; instead, it's the trendy young families that call Setagaya home filling the grassy expanse. This is a park made for locals, where picnickers break bread while the kids kick a soccer ball about. Dotted between them all are nappers and sunbathers embracing the soundtrack and sun.

» Don't leave without checking out the seasonal exhibition at the Setagaya Art Museum on the park grounds.

KIBA PARK

Map 6; enter at the western corner, 4-1 Kiba, Koto;
///declining.topic.earth; www.tokyo-park.or.jp

Split down the middle by a small river, this park aptly attracts two sets of locals: coffee lovers and sporty types. While tennis players enjoy a round on the courts in the east, hip youngsters take it easy at the coffee shops to the west, in the Kiyosumi area. So, which side are you?

UENO PARK

Map 3; enter near Ueno station, Taito; ///chatted.trooper.drive;
(03) 3828-5644

This park is to northeast Tokyoites what Yoyogi is to the central city crew: a spacious public backyard where anything is acceptable, as long as it doesn't interfere with others. This gets trickier in the spring, when the park brims with families and tourists enjoying *hanami* picnic

If it feels too busy, find refuge in Japan's oldest museum, the Tokyo National Museum, in the park. | parties under the iconic cherry blossoms. One of the best places to see the riot of pink, Ueno Park gets lively well into the night, when the blossoms are illuminated.

SHOWA KINEN PARK

Map 6; enter at the Akebono entrance, 3173 Midoricho, Tachikawa; ///grumble.ruffle.deeply; www.showakinen-koen.jp

Like the neighborhood in which it resides, this park is virtually unknown to those who don't live nearby. With an abundance of cycle pathways, Showa Kinen makes for a relaxing weekend bike ride (without having to weave in and out of pedestrian groups). Rent a bike at the entrance gate and stop off at the Rainbow Pool waterpark for a casual dip after all that pedaling.

SHIBA PARK

Map 5; enter near Shibakoen station, 4-10-17 Shibakoen, Minato; ///huddled.parkway.strides; www.tokyo-park.or.jp

A little heavier on the concrete pathways than many of the city's other green spaces, Shiba Park isn't usually the place to stop by for beauty. That all changes in the spring, however, when the resident cherry blossom trees frame postcard-perfect views of Zojoji Temple and Tokyo Tower with soft pink petals. As for the rest of the year you'll only pass salarymen unwrapping their bento boxes and inner-city joggers – but hey, that's the real Tokyo, and still beautiful in its own way.

By the Water

Tokyo may be a concrete jungle, but life is centered around the water – joggers huff along canalside paths, retro boats cruise along the Sumida River, and city slickers welcome the waterfront breeze.

STAND-UP PADDLE BOARDING

Map 6; 3-787-9 Yugimachi, Ome; ///unhinge.highlights.lovably; www.gravity-jp.com

SUPing has taken Tokyo by storm. While most hit the center's waterways to see the city from a new perspective, nature lovers prefer a peaceful paddle on Okutama River. Plenty of companies are in on the action, but Gravity is the best for beginners hoping to follow the flow of mountain streams without falling in (it's part of the fun, mind).

RUN THE ARAKAWA RIVER TRAIL

Map 6; start at Arakawa Sunamachi Tennis Courts; ///skips.settled.whoever

Early marathon trainees and post-work casual joggers chug along to the beat of their headphones up and down this scenic pathway. More suburban sprawl than inner-city adventure, it's an artery into the heart of Tokyo's running scene and the perfect place to get that heart rate up while clocking in a more local side of the city.

TODOROKI VALLEY RIVERSIDE TRAIL

Map 6; 1-22 and 2-37/38 Todoroki, Setagaya; ///refrain.awaiting.heap

A perfectly manicured garden isn't the only way to feel at peace: this untamed, rugged gorge attracts urban explorers looking to lose themselves under the foliage. Follow the elevated walkway along the river to the park's centerpiece, a playhouse-sized red shrine.

» Don't leave without stopping by the shrine's adjacent tearoom for a cup of bitter matcha and piece of *kuzumochi* jelly cake.

ROW DOWN CHIDORIGAFUCHI MOAT

Map 3; Chidorigafuchi Boat Pier, 2-saki Sanbancho, Chiyoda; ///being.fixated.reframe; (03) 3234-1948

Picture Tokyo and you're probably imagining this very activity: couples rowing a boat down a serene waterway while petals fall from cherry blossom trees. In reality, it gets so busy in the spring that you'd have more luck winning big on a *pachinko* machine than scoring a spot for two. Follow those in-the-know and opt for an afternoon out of season – it's no less picturesque (but you might want to keep that a secret).

Try it!
DIP INTO DYEING

The Edo-era art of hand-dyeing has a long connection with the city's waterways. Sign up for a class at Futaba Inc studio *(www. tokyoteshigoto.tokyo)* to learn how art and water shaped the city's textile scene.

Solo, Pair, Crowd

No matter where you are in the city, or who you're with, you'll always find your way to the water.

FLYING SOLO
Take a tour

Part British-style double-decker, part *Transformers* experience, the Skyduck bus-turned-boat-tour takes you around the city's most famous sights both along, and in, the water. It starts from Oshiage.

IN A PAIR
Date with a difference

Want to see the city from a different angle? Hop in a kayak with Tokyo Great Tours, where you'll paddle under iconic bridges and past landmarks. It's a date that will impress.

FOR A CROWD
All aboard

Departing from Odaiba Seaside Park, the sci-fi-esque Jicoo boat turns into a party bar on Thursday, Friday, and Saturday nights, when great DJs and a glistening view of Rainbow Bridge set the mood.

CYCLE THE TAMA RIVER TRAIL

Map 6; start at Numabe Station, Ota; ///shots.guards.graced

The thought of this 29-mile (48-km) uninterrupted path is enough to excite any cyclist, but come the weekend, crowds of walkers and fitness folk put paid to any idea of a serene cycle. Head here in the week instead when it's tranquil and follow along the city's longest river upon a rental bike *(p12)* until you find a patch of greenery to rest.

ODAIBA BEACH

Map 5; Odaiba Marine Park, 1-4 Daiba, Minato;
///kneeled.mini.land; www.tptc.co.jp

Don't let the name fool you: this is most certainly an artificial beach, so much so that swimming is not allowed (though the occasional toe dip is gotten away with). No matter. When the sand's good enough to build a castle or two, who's complaining?

» Don't leave without staying to watch the sunset over the city. It's a great vantage point and a frequent spot for couples on date nights.

DINE ON A YAKATABUNE

Map 3; Houseboat Tokyo cooperative reservation desk, 1-5-10,
Yanagibashi, Taito; ///january.edgy.sweeten; www.yakatabune-kumiai.jp

While bobbing along on a *yakatabune* – a long, retro-style boat – was once reserved for aristocrats, it's a pastime that extends beyond the wealthy today. Friends love these lantern-fringed boats for their central-city views, multi-course dishes, and a little karaoke. Book with Tokyo Yakatabune Association for the addition of free-flowing drinks.

Temples and Shrines

Whoever coined the term "temple fatigue" clearly never visited Tokyo. Testament to the country's rich history and enduring spiritual traditions are sights that ensure a moment of calm is never far away.

SENSOJI TEMPLE

Map 3; start from the Kaminarimon gate and head north, 2-3-1 Asakusa, Taito; ///grain.whizzed.crafted; www.senso-ji.jp

Plastered on every traveler's social media account, this temple is no secret. But the lively atmosphere of the city's most significant and oldest temple is built on the crowds who filter in – especially during the annual Sanja Festival. Celebrating the founders of this temple, Sanja sees portable shrines paraded about the streets, food stalls lining the entrance to the temple, and revelers dancing to drums.

AKAGI SHRINE

Map 3; 1-10 Akagi Motomachi, Shinjuku; ///gold.wicket.limes; www.akagi-jinja.jp

With French music penetrating the grounds and a design direction from Kengo Kuma (who built the 2020 Olympic stadium), this shrine was never going to be a regular site. Overlooked by tourists but loved

Visit later in the day and finish with dinner at the on-site Akagi Café, with a view of the illuminated shrine. by those who live close by, this modern incarnation of a Shinto shrine is a study in architectural innovation and a glimpse of what the future of spirituality could be.

MEIJI SHRINE

Map 2; 1-1 Yoyogikamizonocho, Shibuya; ///glides.clock.waiters;
www.meijijingu.or.jp

A glimpse of older Japan awaits in the grounds of Yoyogi Park *(p168)*. Traditional temple life defines Meiji shrine, where locals perform *harai* (ritual cleansing) before approaching the shrine to pray daily. You may even witness a Japanese wedding, featuring a bride decked out in a pure white kimono with doting entourage in tow.

» Don't leave without writing a wish on an *ema*, a small wooden plaque that's believed to be a direct line to the gods.

ZOJOJI TEMPLE

Map 5; 4-7-35 Shibakoen, Minato;
///entertainer.sanded.finest; www.zojoji.or.jp

Weave around the dressed-up finance workers and bypass the expat-focused sports bars of Roppongi and you'll find this Buddhist temple, proudly backdropped by Tokyo Tower. It's a unique final resting place of the feudal family members of the Tokugawa shogun, nestled as it is between business districts and an iconic landmark, but this poignancy lends it a bit of tranquility in an otherwise bustling district.

NEZU SHRINE

Map 3; 1-28-9 Nezu, Bunkyo; ///gained.reddish.dished; www.nedujinja.or.jp

Angle-savvy snappers crouch for the perfect shot of this shrine, its rows of vermilion *torii* gates resembling Kyoto's iconic Inari Shrine. But unbeknown to them all, an even more photograph-worthy sight fills the grounds from April to May: an azalea festival, where vibrant blooms draw in flower-loving locals.

TOGO SHRINE

Map 1; 1-5-3 Jingumae, Shibuya; ///raves.unable.sampled;
www.togojinja.or.jp

The city's perfect harmony of chaos and tranquility could hardly be embodied any better than at Togo Shrine, a peaceful spot just behind Harajuku's hectic main drag. Office workers taking the after-lunch shortcut and fashionable moms pushing their children in SUV-level strollers make up the majority of the foot traffic here, where taking a pause from hectic city life is pretty mandatory.

YASUKUNI SHRINE

Map 3; 3-1-1 Kudankita, Chiyoda; ///trickle.last.horn;
www.yasukuni.or.jp

Considered the country's most controversial landmark, this regal shrine was the creation of Emperor Meiji who, in an arguably egotistical move, built the structure as a homage to the millions who lost their lives defending him during the tumultuous Meiji era. It's a sobering place to visit at any time, though the spring sees a renewed spirit with the welcoming of the cherry blossom season. If you choose to brave it in the spring, expect crowds drinking, dancing, and eating among beautiful blossoms.

GOTOKUJI TEMPLE
Map 6; 2-24-7 Gotokuji, Setagaya; ///knots.admiringly.rashers; www.gotokuji.jp

There's arguably no other nation with a stronger affinity for the feline than Japan – so much so that Tokyo is home to a "lucky cat" temple. An unusual place, it's populated by thousands of white-pawed waving *maneki neko* figurines (the type you see outside Asian restaurants) that have been offered up by visitors. Relatively unknown within mainstream tourist circles, Gotokuji is famous locally with cat lovers who could tell you a thing or two about *maneki neko* origins (like the fact that it's Japanese, not Chinese as many mistakenly believe).

» Don't leave without purchasing your very own lucky kitty. Whether you take it home or offer it up to the temple after saying a prayer is up to you, though it's polite to bring it back if your wish comes true.

Try it!
CRAFT A CAT

Make your very own *maneki neko* as you munch on a cat-shaped doughnut at Nekoemon Café *(5-4-2 Yanaka, Taito)*, one of the many feline-themed shops around Yanaka, Tokyo's unofficial "cat town."

Nearby Getaways

Locals love to bask in Tokyo's energy, but sometimes the sea breeze or mountain air brings welcome respite. With the promise of unique day trips close by, there's no reason to resist getting out of town.

HAKONE

1.5 hours from Tokyo Station; www.hakone-japan.com

No matter how soothing Tokyo's *onsen* are, there's nothing quite like getting close to nature while relaxing in a steaming bath – and that's exactly why locals flock to this hot springs resort town. You won't find concrete-clad landscapes here: just views of Lake Ashi and Mount

Fuji from the many *onsen* and *ryokan* (traditional inns). This is the trip that groups roll out for a bit of R&R – a weekend getaway with the girls or a daytime bath to soak away the aches of the working week.

» Don't leave without taking the Hakone Ropeway, an aerial lift that offers even more incredible views of the area and Mount Fuji.

KAWAGOE

1 hour from Shinjuku Station; www.koedo.or.jp

Picture this: kimono-clad locals, tranquil streets peppered with claywalled *kura* buildings, street-food vendors selling sweet-potato snacks, a historic bell tower ringing four times a day. Welcome to "Little Edo," as the locals call it. Time seems to stand still at this town, which preserves a 19th-century atmosphere, and that's exactly why urbanites descend upon it when ultramodern Tokyo feels too, well, modern. Immersing yourself in tradition has never been so easy.

CHICHIBU

2 hours from Shinjuku Station

Ask anyone with a penchant for spirituality where to get in touch with your inner calm and they'll send you here. This town is famed for the Chichibu 34 Kannon Pilgrimage, a 60-mile (100-km) path that links 34 temples. If you don't have four days to spare journeying along the route, though, make like the locals and pick one temple to visit. Hint: Taiyo-ji, high in the mountains, is one of the few of the 34 temples still run by a Buddhist monk, who helps you zone out from life's pressures with meditation sessions and some natural healing. And breathe.

YOKOHAMA

20 minutes from Tokyo Station; www.yokohamajapan.com

If young Tokyo locals could live in any other Japanese city, they'd choose Yokohama – a creative hub, with artists and entrepreneurs shaping every corner. And just think, if you did move, you'd have all this on your doorstep: the street-food offerings at Japan's largest Chinatown, the shopping hot spot of Red Brick Warehouse, the view of ships going in and out of the vibrant port, and a latticework of artists' studios underneath the Keikyu railroad tracks.

KAMAKURA

1 hour from Shinagawa Station

As soon as summer hits the capital, everyone has only one place in mind to escape the humidity: this quaint seaside town, complete with a much-needed sea breeze. Spending time here feels like being on holiday, where families, friends, and couples while away days sunbathing on the sandy beaches, shopping for souvenirs in the bustling town, and sightseeing around the many temples and shrines.

MOUNT FUJI

2 hours from Shinjuku Station

This Japanese icon needs no introduction. While you can spot its cone floating in the distance from Tokyo on clear days, nothing beats seeing it close up. Those with a head for heights climb to the summit, but most of the locals who day-trip out here stay firmly on the ground, exploring the Fuji Five Lakes instead. Head to the small

Visit Fuji Q Highland theme park on your way to Mount Fuji and enjoy the famous roller coasters.

lake towns surrounding the base of the mountain for some epic vantage points (Lake Kawaguchiko and Lake Ashi, to be precise).

OKUTAMA

2 hours from Shinjuku Station

The forested region of Okutama is fast becoming the go-to place for those craving the great outdoors. And it's easy to see why: colorful caves, relaxing hot springs, and magnificent waterfalls fill this natural paradise. Come the weekend, thrillseekers immerse themselves in the water, donning a helmet to zipline over the river, slide down waterfalls, and swim between canyons. Afterward, they reward their efforts by sinking a reviving pint in one of the town's beer breweries.

» Don't leave without fishing at the Hikawa International Trout Fishing spot. The staff at the BBQ house nearby will even cook your catch.

MOUNT TAKAO

50 minutes from Shinjuku Station

It's fair to say that avid hikers aren't spoiled for choice within Tokyo, so when they're itching for a thigh-screaming adventure, Mount Takao provides just that. A hike up isn't just about reaching the top (though the views at the summit are impeccable). The path winds past scenic temples, shrines, and even the odd *soba* restaurant. After you've taken it all in, follow the locals to the resident *onsen* at the foot of the mountain and soak those tired muscles. A day well spent.

A morning exploring
idyllic Ueno Park

Ask any local which park is their favorite and, chances are, they'll pick Ueno. Why? It's practically a mini city, home to temples, lakes, museums, lively markets – the list goes on. Given its popularity, it gets pretty busy in the afternoons, when street entertainers are out in full force and workers spread out picnic rugs on their lunch breaks. It's much more peaceful in the morning, so start the day early and wander through at a leisurely pace, though that morning may well turn into a full day – heck, there's enough to keep you busy here.

NEZU

HONGO

1. Tokyo National Museum
13-9 Uenokoen, Taito;
www.tnm.jp
///dunes.lunges.rams

2. EVERYONEs CAFE
8-4 Uenokoen,
Taito; www.create-
restaurants.co.jp
///amused.communal.keep

**3. Kiyomizu
Kannon-do Temple**
1-29 Uenokoen, Taito
///inferior.goggles.drips

4. Ameya Yokocho Market
4-10-10 Ueno, Taito;
www.ameyoko.net
///property.audible.price

5. University of Tokyo
7-3-1 Hongo, Bunkyo;
www.u-tokyo.ac.jp/en/
///unions.gulped.warrior

📍 **Ueno Daibutsu**
///dividing.musician.analogy

📍 **Shinobazu Pond**
///calculating.mile.smoker

**Snoop at the
UNIVERSITY
OF TOKYO** 5
You can't go inside, but the exterior is divine enough. Admire the architecture and verdant surrounds while energetic students flit between campus and the neighboring park.

Yanaka
Cemetery

NEGISHI

YANAKA

UENO-
SAKURAGI

KOTOTOI - DORI

Dip into the
TOKYO NATIONAL
MUSEUM

Hit up Japan's oldest
museum when it opens
(9:30am), and spend an
hour exploring the Honkan
gallery for an introduction
to Japanese heritage.

1

In the center lies **Ueno
Daibutsu**, *a disembodied
head of a bronze Buddha
statue. It's believed to
be a good luck symbol
for students.*

Ueno
Park

IKENOHATA

SHINOBAZU - DORI

2

Take a break at
EVERYONEs CAFE

Pull up a chair under the trees
at this modern spot and enjoy
a herbal tea with a side of
people-watching.

3

Swing by
KIYOMIZU
KANNON-DO TEMPLE

Admire the oddly shaped pine tree
in front of this temple, then soak in
the views over Shinobazu Pond.

HIGASHI-
UENO

*Shinobazu
Pond*

MUEN-ZAKA

*Kyu-Iwasaki-
Tei Gardens*

CHUO - DORI

4

Mooch around
AMEYA YOKOCHO
MARKET

Pop out of the gates to this
vibrant market, picking up
some supplies from the
international food stalls to set
up a picnic back in the park.

*You might just recognize
Shinobazu Pond with
its famously oversized lily
pads; it's a star of
the city's landscape-
painting scene.*

UENO

YUSHIMA

| 0 meters | 300 |
| 0 yards | 300 |

With a little research and preparation, this city will feel like a home away from home. Check out these websites to ensure a healthy, safe stay in Tokyo.

Tokyo
DIRECTORY

SAFE SPACES

Tokyo is a friendly and inclusive city, but should you feel uneasy at any point or want to find your community, there are supportive spaces to turn to.

www.jccjapan.jp
The Jewish Community of Japan, running congregations and events in Tokyo.

www.legacyfoundationjapan.com
Information and resources on finding Black communities in Japan.

www.pridehouse.jp
Counseling and information for the LGBTQ+ community.

www.stonewalljapan.org
Connecting Japan's LGBTQ+ community through online platforms and events.

www.telljp.com
Mental health support and counseling services for Japan's expat and international communities.

HEALTH

Health care in Japan isn't free, so it's important to take out comprehensive health insurance for your visit. If you do need medical assistance, there are many pharmacies and hospitals across the city.

www.himawari.metro.tokyo.jp
Pharmacy and medical institution search network with a multilingual hotline.

www.hospital.luke.ac.jp
One of Tokyo's largest hospitals, right in the city center.

www.mhlw.go.jp
Government health ministry services.

www.national-azabu.com
International supermarket and English-friendly pharmacy.

www.reiko-dental.com
English-friendly dental clinic in Akasaka.

TRAVEL SAFETY ADVICE

Before you travel – and while you're here – always keep tabs on the latest regulations in Tokyo and Japan.

www.keishicho.metro.tokyo.lg.jp
Information from the Tokyo Metropolitan Police Department, including a list of stations in the city.

www.japan.go.jp
Latest travel safety information from the Japanese government.

www.japan.travel
Japan National Tourism Organization, with updates on COVID-19 and an English-speaking visitor helpline.

www.jma.go.jp
Weather forecasts and advisories, including typhoon alerts.

www.metro.tokyo.lg.jp
Includes an Earthquake Survival Manual should a strong tremor happen.

www.soudanplus.jp
A helpline providing support and resources for victims of domestic abuse.

ACCESSIBILITY

Tokyo has come a long way when it comes to accessibility, though some ancient temples can prove tricky for wheelchair users. These resources will help make your journeys go smoothly.

www.accessible-japan.com
Planning resources for those with specific requirements, including accessible attractions and tours, as well as transportation.

www.japan-accessible.com
Tokyo travel tips for wheelchair users, organized by area.

www.ecomo-rakuraku.jp
Search tool showing accessibility levels in stations across Japan.

www.odekakeoffice.jp
Accessible taxi service, with wheelchair lifts, across the city.

www.nittento.or.jp
Japan Braille Library, providing Japanese Braille lessons and counseling for those with visual impairments.

INDEX

ACKNOWLEDGMENTS

Meet the illustrator

*Award-winning British illustrator
David Doran is based in a studio by
the sea in Falmouth, Cornwall. When
not drawing and designing, David tries
to make the most of the beautiful area
in which he's based; sea-swimming all
year round, running the coastal paths
and generally spending as much time
outside as possible.*

With thanks

*DK Eyewitness would like to thank the
following people for their contribution to
the first edition of this book: Lucy Dayman,
Kaila Imada, Lucy Richards, Tania Gomes,
Zoë Rutland, and Casper Morris.*

THIS EDITION UPDATED BY

Contributors Lucy Dayman, Kaila Imada
Senior Editor Zoë Rutland
Project Art Editor Bandana Paul
Designer Jordan Lambley
Senior Cartographic Editor Casper Morris
Cartography Manager Suresh Kumar
Jacket Designer Sarah Snelling
Jacket Illustrator David Doran
Senior DTP Designer Tanveer Zaidi
Senior Production Editor Jason Little
Senior Production Controller Samantha Cross
Managing Editor Hollie Teague
Managing Art Editors Sarah Snelling,
Priyanka Thakur
Art Director Maxine Pedliham
Publishing Director Georgina Dee

First edition 2021

Published in Great Britain by Dorling Kindersley Limited,
DK, One Embassy Gardens, 8 Viaduct Gardens,
London SW11 7BW.

The authorised representative in the EEA is
Dorling Kindersley Verlag GmbH. Arnulfstr. 124,
80636 Munich, Germany.

Published in the United States by DK Publishing,
1745 Broadway, 20th Floor, New York, NY 10019, USA.

Copyright © 2021, 2023 Dorling Kindersley Limited
A Penguin Random House Company
22 23 24 25 10 9 8 7 6 5 4 3 2 1

All rights reserved.

The publishers cannot accept responsibility for any consequences arising from
the use of this book, nor for any material on third party websites, and cannot
guarantee that any website address in this book will be a suitable source of
travel information.

A CIP catalog record for this book is available from the British Library.

A catalog record for this book is available from the Library of Congress.

ISSN: 1542 1554
ISBN: 978 0 2415 69061

Printed and bound in China.

www.dk.com

MIX
Paper | Supporting
responsible forestry
FSC™ C018179
www.fsc.org

This book was made with
Forest Stewardship Council™
certified paper – one small step
in DK's commitment to a
sustainable future.
**For more information go to
www.dk.com/our-green-pledge**

A NOTE FROM DK EYEWITNESS

The world is fast-changing and it's keeping us folk at
DK Eyewitness on our toes. We've worked hard to ensure
that this edition of Tokyo Like a Local is up-to-date and
reflects today's favourite places but we know that standards
shift, venues close, and new ones pop up in their place. So, if
you notice something has closed, we've got something
wrong or left something out, we want to hear about it.
Please drop us a line at travelguides@dk.com